Singer's Repertoire

Part V:
Program Notes for the Singer's Repertoire

Second Edition

Berton Coffin and
Werner Singer

The Scarecrow Press, Inc.
Lanham, Maryland • Toronto • Oxford
2005

SCARECROW PRESS, INC.

Published in the United States of America
by Scarecrow Press, Inc.
A wholly owned subsidiary of The Rowman & Littlefield Publishing Group, Inc.
4501 Forbes Boulevard, Suite 200, Lanham, Maryland 20706
www.scarecrowpress.com

PO Box 317
Oxford
OX2 9RU, UK

British Library Cataloguing in Publication Information Available

Library of Congress Control Number: 60-7265

ISBN 0-8108-5422-8 (pbk. : alk. paper)

To
Paola Novikova

My beloved wife whose wise guidance
and faith made this book possible.

W. S.

To
Paola Novikova

My esteemed vocal master and cherished
friend.

B. C.

Foreword

Singing has been defined by the late William J. Henderson, eminent vocal critic and authority, as being "the interpretation of a text by means of musical tones produced by the human voice." A knowledge of the text, as it was in the song's creation, should be the first point of song interpretation, and, for deepest appreciation, should be available to audiences. For as entertainment media are becoming more entrancing and colorful, so must performances on the lyric stage. This can only be done by convincingly strengthening the inner meanings of the lyric repertoire by the performer, and by conveying those meanings to the audience through the voice and by the use of appropriately interpretative program notes. In this country, lamentably mono-lingual, it is necessary that audiences be informed of the essence of the foreign language texts. With the public demanding, both those present and those absent, that they should know more about the values of lyric performances, it is mandatory that all programs be assisted by the use of program notes.

"Program Notes for the Singer's Repertoire" has been designed for use by professional singers, amateur singers, teachers, coaches and students. The singer, with the pressures of contemporary life, frequently cannot take the time to do the necessary research on songs and to place that information in program notes of a literary form comparable to the artistic values of his recital appearances.

For all persons concerned in any way with the singing art, this book may also be used as a means of becoming acquainted with the basic vocal repertoire. The difference in the amount of time necessary for the acquaintance of poetic and musical values is astounding. These program notes for more than 1,000 songs and arias can be read in less than a week, but the hearing of the music would take much longer. The authors therefore feel that one of their greatest contributions has been made in providing an easier overview of the basic vocal repertoire. Possibly these program notes will also assist singers in thinking more of their art as poetry wedded to a reflecting melody and vocal color.

In addition to use as a technique of choosing a repertoire, this book may further be considered a valuable aid in program building, for the desired contrasts in a program are concerned with a variety of literary ideas, as well as a cognizance of the various colors of the music.

This book, which becomes Volume V in the "Singer's Repertoire" series, is an outgrowth of the expressed desires of many singers and teachers that the "Singer's Repertoire" include annotations of the listed songs. We have been fortunate in securing the collaboration of Werner Singer of New York City, who has had a wealth of experience in the concert and operatic field. German-born, he was trained at the Staatliche Hochschule für Musik, Berlin and has conducted operas at the Hamburg Volksoper and the Theatro Municipal, Rio de Janeiro, Brazil. In this country he is widely known, having been a coach and/or accompanist to Mmes. Barbieri, Berger, Leider, Loevberg, Tebaldi and Yeend, and Messrs. Bernac, de Luca, Gedda, London, Svanholm, Tagliavini, Tauber and Vinay. In the academic field, Mr. Singer has established and has been successfully holding summer classes in "Repertoire for Singers" at the University of Colorado.

For many years Mr. Singer has written and collected program notes. These have been supplemented by materials which have been collected in the first and second editions of the "Singer's Repertoire." Further translations of important songs have been made so that the songs and arias in this work are representative of the Classic, Romantic, Impressionistic, Modern and Neo-classic schools of composition in foreign languages.

The format of this book is alphabetical by composer, with the alphabetical listing of program notes following. There is an index to song titles and an index to composers. The significant song composers have short descriptive paragraphs in their first entries, which will give information about their styles and vocal contributions. This information may be used in other program notes of the same composer as supplementary material. Repetitions have been omitted in the program notes and the translated lyrics reduced to the essential poetic thought.

It is felt that the songs annotated in this volume represent the basic songs and arias in the French, German, Italian, Russian, Spanish, Portuguese and Norwegian lyric repertoires. Actually over sixty recitals could be given from these songs without a single repetition!

Berton Coffin
Boulder, Colorado.
October 22, 1960

Villanella (Country song) Acqua
   This is a country song in which a girl sings of a swallow
   flying through the clear blue of morning, as to the land
   of Apollo and sunshine.

The nightingale. Alabieff
   Nightingale, where do you sing at break of day? Sing
   and tell him of my heart's deep sadness.

Perchè siedi là (Why are you sitting there?) Alfano
   Why are you sitting there tinkling your bracelets? Fill
   your pail. It is time for you to go home. Why are you
   splashing the water with your hands - always looking toward the road to see if someone is coming? Why do
   you tarry? Fill your pail and come home. The clouds
   gather behind the hill. They seem to pause - looking in
   your face and smiling. Do not tarry - fill your pail and
   come home!

Aminte (18th century) Anonymous
   Come with me, Aminte. Life is made for pleasure. In
   shadows of the forest let us make a tender homage to
   love.

Amor, fammi goder (Amor, make me happy) 17th century
Anonymous
   Amor, make me happy! Let me kiss those red lips
   which you use as a bow, you archer with the blind on
   your eyes!

Dites, que faut-il faire? (Tell me, what must one do?)
Anonymous
   Tell me, what must be done to keep one's heart ever
   true? Must one smile or sigh demurely? To confess
   to love is not best.

Lamentation napolitaine (Neapolitan lament) 17th Century
Anonymous
   Let him weep who sees my suffering. My pain deserves
   pity. I no longer have joy and cheerfulness, and I no
   longer see the sun. Fate is angry with me. Death and
   the tomb claim me. I shall never say why.

9

L'amour de moi (My love) 15th century Anonymous
My love is a little garden where roses, lilies of the valley and hollyhocks grow. This garden is beautiful - pleasant and full of flowers. One enjoys it as much in daytime as during the night. But the sweetest thing is the nightingale which sings in the evening and in the morning. One day I picked violets and looked at them. They were white as milk, soft as a lamb, and fresh as roses

Le tambourin (The tambourine) 18th century Anonymous
Come into the woods, beloved, the place is made for pleasure and play. The birds are singing - the murmuring waters are inviting us to render sweet homage to the god of love.

Quant li rossignol (When the nightingale) 12th century Anonymous
When the nightingale sings, and the rose and lily bloom, then should the lover offer his song of love.

Preach not me your musty rules, from "Comus" Arne
Milton's "Comus" is far removed from the austere Puritanism generally associated with his poetry. It is a masque of riotous pleasure, built on the thesis, "They only live who life enjoy." Henry Lawes, a contemporary of Milton, first set some of these verses to music, and later, Dr. Arne, the composer of "Rule, Britannia," accomplished the task even more successfully.

BACH
Bach has been described as a mystic in the true sense of the word, who, by contemplation and self-surrender, sought to obtain union with his Deity. Most of his vocal works are of a religious nature in which a deeply devotional spirit is present. As a great polyphonic composer, even the solo voice is treated as an instrumental line in the fabric of music. Extreme difficulties are presented to the singer since the phrases do not always lie well for the voice.

Bist du bei mir (If you are with me) Bach
If you are with me, I gladly die and go to my rest. How joyful my end would be if your beloved hands closed my eyes.

Es ist vollbracht (It is accomplished) Bach
It is accomplished... The Lord hath freed me from earthly sins... Let me offer thanks to Him.

Good fellows, be merry, from "Peasant Cantata"   Bach
Bach wrote the Peasant Cantata for a friend on the oc-
casion of his taking over a new estate.   Despite its severe classic form, the air shows the composer in a jovi-
al mood.

Komm, süsser Tod (Come, sweet death)   Bach
Come sweet death; come welcome guest!   From worldly
strife I repose.   As my eyelids gently close, I wait for
thee.   Come thou, be my guide.

Chère nuit   (Dear night)   Bachelet
Twilight is here.   I hear the song of all creation and
the sweet perfume of flowers enfolds me.   Dear night,
cover the earth with thy mysterious charm, for the joys
of love are reborn beneath thy wings.

Mot Kveld   (Toward evening)   Backer-Grondahl
Flowers, covered with dew, bid the sun adieu.   Glow-
worms glisten on the bushes; butterflies, in their coats
of dew, dream of joyous days and fragrant violets, as
they nestle in the cup of the blue bell.

Then you'll remember me, from "The Bohemian Girl"   Balfe
The never-failing melodic charm of "The Bohemian Girl"
is not Bohemian but Celtic in origin, for the composer
was born in Dublin, in 1808.   Of his many operas this is
the most famous.

In Act III, Arline, the heroine, has been restored to her
father, the Count, from whom she had been stolen in her
infancy by a band of strolling gypsies.   Secretly she
meets her gypsy lover who, with this song, recalls their
former happiness.

BEETHOVEN
Beethoven, in his seventy-nine songs, contributed many
innovations on which, alone, his fame could endure.   His
"An die ferne Geliebte" was the first song cycle, and his
"Adelaide" can be considered as one of the first concert
arias.   Both developments were outgrowths of his love
for breadth and sweep in the larger musical forms.   Another of the larger works is Opus 48, "Gellert Lieder,"
a group of songs intensely religious in nature.   His vocal
lines are not always gracious for the voice, for his revolutionary musical genius could not always be confined to
the limitations of the instruments for which he wrote.

11

Abscheulicher! Wo eilst du hin? (Leonore's Aria) from
"Fidelio" Beethoven
  Inhuman! What next? Neither pity nor mercy can
  change your hateful mind? Come, Hope, let me reach
  the far away goal. Love will give me strength. Could
  I only bring consolation to my beloved husband, imprisoned by the Inhuman's malice!

Adelaide Beethoven
  Your lonely friend wanders through the countryside, but
  your image accompanies him, Adelaide! A flower will
  grow on my grave, nourished by the ashes of my heart,
  and each little leaf will be inscribed with your name:
  Adelaide!

Ah! Perfido (Ah, Traitor) Beethoven
  Ah, traitor, you desert me? The cruel words of farewell have wounded my heart! Go and leave me, but the
  rage of the Gods will follow you! In dreams I see
  flames and lightnings punishing the perfidious! Oh, no!
  spare him, raging Gods! I lived for him, so let me die
  for him! Without him, I cannot live.

An Die Ferne Geliebte (To The Beloved, So Far Away)
Beethoven
1. Sitting by the side of the hill, I look down into the valley
   where I met my beloved one. She is so far away, mountains and valleys separate us and deny us our happiness.
   You cannot see my thoughts which I send to you, cannot
   hear the sighing. Is there no messenger of my love?
   I shall sing and the songs will tell you of my suffering.
   Songs do not know distance nor time; they are the bridge
   from one loving heart to another.

2. I would like to be where the blue mountains are and
   where the sun sets! Nothing would keep me here, could
   I be united with you forever!

3. You birds in the heights, you little brook, if you see my
   beloved, greet her many thousand times. Tell her of my
   longing and tears!

4. The birds and the clouds will see you from above - could
   they take me with them! The winds will caress your
   cheeks and bosom, and play with your silken hair - could
   I only take part!

5. Spring is here with its gentle breezes. The swallow returns and builds a nest where love shall reside, and pairs

12

are united after the winter's separation. Spring helps
everyone who is in love - but me.

6. Receive my songs, beloved, which come from a loving
    heart and tell you of my longing. Sing them back in the
    evening and heart will speak to heart!

Der Floh (The flea) Beethoven
    Long ago a king lived who kept a pet flea and cherished
    him as dearly as a son. He sent for his tailor and
    clothed him in velvet, and give him a jeweled order, too.
    Ha! Ha! He made him a minister and gave him a dia-
    mond to wear. All of his relatives were given highest
    orders. Ha! Ha! The courtiers were no longer gay, for
    they were pestered by fleas, both night and day. They
    were forbidden to scratch, no matter how much they were
    bitten. But we can scratch and kick when we are bitten!
    Ha! Ha!!

Die Ehre Gottes aus der Natur (Nature honoring God)
Beethoven
    The heavens tell the glory of God, as far as the stars
    are shining. Air, earth and seas repeat the same story.
    Hear, O man, the voice divine. Who makes the number-
    less stars of the heavens? Who, from His throne, guides
    the sun? It appears and shines and laughs from afar and
    goes its path as a hero.

Lieder des Klärchen aus Goethes "Egmont" Beethoven
1. Die Trommel gerühret (Let the drum beat)
    Let the drum beat and the fife play. My sweetheart, in
    armor and with lifted lance, sways the crowd and rules
    the land. Oh, that I might in armor join him as he
    goes through provinces high and low. The enemy flees
    with us on their heels. What a joy to be a man!

2. Freudvoll und leidvoll (Joyful and sorrowful)
    Happiness and sorrow, longing and pain...joy comes only
    to the soul who loves.

Gott! Welch Dunkel hier! (Florestan's Aria), from "Fidelio"
Beethoven
    God! What darkness, what cruel silence! No living
    creature here but me. What heavy trial! But God is
    just, His will be done. They put me in chains for having
    said the truth. My end is near but sweet consolation
    fills my heart: I've done my duty. - What light falls in-
    to my grave? I see a consoling angel beside me: an
    angel, Leonore, my wife, she leads me to freedom -

13

to heaven!

Ich liebe dich (I love you)   Beethoven
I love you, as you love me.   We shared our worries and
divided our cares.   You comforted me when in grief,
and my tears dissolved your sorrow.   May God bless
you, and protect both of us.

In questa tomba oscura (In the tomb's darkness) Beethoven
Let me sleep in the darkness of this tomb; while I was
alive, you should have cared for me, unfaithful one!

Mignon   Beethoven
Do you know the land where the citron blows, where in
the leafy shade burns the golden orange?   Do you
know that house of gleaming halls and chambers: the
cloud-enshrouded mount where dragons lurk?   Oh, I
would go there with you!

Mit einem gemalten Band (With a painted ribbon) Beethoven
Spring presents me with roses which I attach to a light
ribbon.   Zephyr shall carry the ribbon to my beloved and
adorn her dress with it.   If she sees herself in the mirror, surrounded by roses, she will look like a rosebud.
She will feel my heart longing for her and be mine!
That which will unite us shall not be a weak ribbon of
roses.

Wonne der Wehmut (Joy of sorrow)   Beethoven
Dry not, dry not, tears of eternal love.   Dry not!   Ah,
how cold and dead the world seems to the half-dried eye.
Dry not, dry not, tears of lost love.

Ah! Per sempre (Ah! Forever), from "I Puritani" Bellini
In one of Bellini's truly magnificent arias from Act I of
"I Puritani," Ricardo sings sadly of his great love for
Elvira which will never again be returned because her
love is for another.   "Ah! I have lost you forever, my
only love."

Casta diva (Pure Goddess), from "Norma" Bellini
A prayer in which Norma, the Druid Princess, invokes
the moon goddess to extend the peace of the skies to the
troubled earth.

L'absence (Absence)   Berlioz
Come back, my beloved.   Like a flower without sun, the
flower of my life is unopened without your rosy smile.
What distance lies between our hearts!   What space lies

between our kisses! O bitter fate, o cruel absence! O
great desires unappeased! Come back my beloved!

La mort de Cléopatre (The death of Cleopatra)   Berlioz
The scene consists of three arias, ranging from antique
declamation in Gluck's style, to the Shakespearean vision
of Cleopatra, dreaming that her shade greets those of
all the Ptolemies. This section bears a motto from
''Romeo and Juliet...'' ''How if when I am laid in the
tomb...'' The last section is a death scene, somewhat
suggestive of the love-potion music from Tristan, thirty
years later. Berlioz used several of the Cleopatra
themes in his mélologue, "Lelio."

Méphisto's serenade, from "La Damnation de Faust" Berlioz
After Faust has entered Marguerite's house, Méphis-
tophélès sings this mocking serenade:

Why, fair maid, wilt you loiter in the shade by the door
of your lover? Though the darkness may cover your
blushes, have a care! and be good! Heed this one thing,
would you escape your undoing - quench the thirst of his
wooing with a, "First, if it pleases you, the ring."

Fanciullo mendico (The beggar boy)   Bettarini
The lyric describes the memory of a meeting with a
poor suffering child who will not accept pity. The child's
mother is dead and the child is without bread.

Echo song   Bishop
This famous English composer and conductor was knighted
in 1842. He wrote many works of varied dimensions,
and also made adaptations from other composers. The
Echo Song is a favorite with coloratura singers and re-
quires a fine command of vocalism.

BIZET
Bizet is primarily known for his opera, "Carmen," written three months before his untimely death at thirty-
seven years of age. He had previously written several
operas which have been performed without notable success. "Carmen," characterized by vital rhythms, unusual harmonies and orchestral color, may be considered a
verismo opera since it is based upon the extreme realism
of a sordid and brutal subject, rather than one based on
an inspirational theme.

Adieu de l'hôtesse Arabe (Farewell of the Arabian guest) Bizet
Since nothing will detain you in this beautiful land, alas,
farewell, handsome traveler! If you do not return, perhaps you will recall with nostalgia, the girls of the desert,
my sweet-voiced sisters who dance barefoot on the Dunes.
O, handsome, white stranger, bird of passage, remember - for more than one of us will remember you.

Agnus Dei (Lamb of God) Bizet
Lamb of God, who taketh away the sins of the world,
Have mercy upon us and give us peace.

Au fond du temple saint (On the steps of the temple), from
"Les Pêcheurs de Perles" Bizet
Zurga and Nadir, two fishermen of the island of Ceylon,
meet and swear eternal friendship, resolved to forget
that long ago they quarreled over a beautiful priestess in
the temple of Brahma. The next moment, they are ap-
proached by a procession accompanying a veiled priestess,
and Nadir recognizes her as the subject of the old quarrel. He realizes that he is still in love with her. She
enters the temple, the people disperse, and Nadir is
left alone to dream of the night he followed her to a secret retreat and listened to her singing. In this aria, he
recalls that experience and the vision of beauty, revealed
when the night wind swept aside her veils.

Chanson de toreador (Toreador's song) from "Carmen" Bizet
Escamillo, being toasted by army officers, replies that
he understands their life, for toreadors also fight and
flirt with death. He then describes a bull-fight.

Habanera, from "Carmen" Bizet
Love is like a rebellious bird who knows no law. You
can call him all you want, but if he does not want to
hear you, threatenings or prayers are of no avail.

Pastorale Bizet
Colin, the shepherd lad, wishes to steal a kiss from his
"bergère." "Non, non, non," she sings, "you need not
steal what I will give you."

Je crois entendre encore (I believe I still hear), from "Les
Pêcheurs de Perles" Bizet
Bizet's fondness for exotic subjects is displayed in "The
Pearl Fishers," with its setting on the shores of Ceylon.
Nadir recognizes the priestess, Leila, as his love in
disguise, and passionately declares his love! "Oh, en-
chanted night, gloriously divine! Oh, memories so

charming, joys that pass like dreams!"

Je dis que riens (I say nothing will frighten me), from
"Carmen"   Bizet
    Here is the refuge of the smugglers.   He is here; I
shall see him.   The task his mother imposed on me, I
will fulfill without trembling.   I say that nothing will
frighten me; I say, alas, that I can rely on myself.
But, although I pretend to be courageous, at the bottom
of my heart, I am dying of terror.   Alone in this wild
place, I am afraid; but it is wrong of me, for Thou wilt
give me courage and protect me, oh Lord.   I will see
this woman who, with her bad influence, has made the
one that I loved an infamous man.   She is dangerous,
she is beautiful, but I will not be afraid.   I will hold my
head before her.   Lord, Thou wilt protect me.

La fleur que tu m'avai jetée (The flower you have thrown me),
from "Carmen"   Bizet
    Don José reminds Carmen of the flower she threw to him
at their first meeting, and, in touching accents, tells
how he kept it through the dreary weeks of his prison
life.   He closes with, "Oh, my Carmen, I lived only for
you.   Carmen, I love you."

Duet: Parle-moi de ma mère (Tell me of my mother), from
"Carmen"   Bizet
    Micaela finds José in the market place and says she has
a message from his mother.   She brings him money and
a kiss, and implores him to return again to his beloved
village.   In the charming duet, José sings of the joy of
returning to his childhood surroundings and his aged
mother.

Près des ramparts de Seville (Seguidilla.   Near to the walls
of Seville), from "Carmen"   Bizet
    Carmen, under arrest for the knifing of a fellow worker
in the factory, sings of a rendevous she intends to make
with Don José at a tavern outside of Seville, owned by
her friend, Lilas Pastia.

Still wie die Nacht (Calm as the night)   Bohm
    Calm as the night and deep as the sea, your love should
be!   If your love is as fervent and firm as mine, I will
be yours!

Lontano, lontano (Far, far away), from "Mefistofele"   Boito
    Long before Gounod produced his opera Faust, based on
Goethe's great dramatic poem, Boito was working on the

17

same theme. However, the first performance at La
Scala in 1868 was a failure, due to the composer's inex-
perience in dramatic writing. But in the revised production, given seven years later in Bologna, the many beauties of the score won for it the recognition it deserves.
This is the duet between Faust and Marguerite in the
third act, declaring undying love for each other.

L'altra notte (The other night), from "Mefistofele"   Boito
The other night, they took my child and threw it into the
sea; and now they say I drowned it. In this cold and
dark prison, my soul is flying away like a sparrow in
the forest. Have mercy. My mother is in deep sleep,
and they say I have poisoned her. What horror!

A dissonance   Borodin
Your lips say, "I love you," but falseness is in your
voice, smile and eyes. You know that you cannot deceive me.

Aria of Prince Igor, from "Prince Igor"   Borodin
No sleep, no rest for my tortured soul. The night does
not send forgetfulness. All the past I relive again, and
I see God's sign of warning. Great fame, my victory
over the enemy and glory – all come to a bitter end. I
have lost my faithful army for my country – all is lost.
Prison, shameful prison! All blame me for the destiny
of my country. O, give me my freedom and I shall save
my honor and free Russia. My darling, you alone do
not reproach me. While weeping and waiting for me you
understand and will forgive. Must I be imprisoned while
the enemy tortures Russia? I shall save Russia, but the
night sends no hope – only the past and its heavy burdens.

Prince Vladimir's Aria, from "Prince Igor"   Borodin
Now twilight descends and night spreads her silent wings.
Gentle night, bring the hour of meeting with my love.
How slow the moments of waiting. The hour has come
at last for our tender greeting.

The sleeping Princess   Borodin
Hush! A Princess lies asleep under a fairy charm.
Suddenly, the elves break the silence with laughing and
shouting, but she does not wake. They say that some
day a Prince will wake her with a kiss. Will she ever
wake? Who can tell!

BRAHMS
Brahms, who was accompanist to many of the finest

18

Lieder singers of his time, had a superb knowledge of
the voice as an instrument, which is evident in all of his
194 songs for solo voice. His melodic line was influenced by his interest in folk songs, of which he made
49 arrangements; his harmonies are usually rich in color.
His songs are not illustrations of the words, but are
basically moods founded on the sentiment of the lyrics,
with the melody being of first importance. He was a
master of long, sweeping lines and the interpreter of his
songs must be a master of the sustained legato. His
music is characterized by profound thought and deep emotion.

Ach, wende diesen Blick (Ah do not look at me)   Brahms
Ah, do not look at me! Do not fill my soul again with
an ever new passsion. Even when my tortured soul is at
rest, one fleeting glance from you awakens pain that
stirs my heart like a serpent!

Alte Liebe (Old love)   Brahms
The swallows and storks return from far countries and
bring with them the nostalgia of spring, while my heart
is heavy with the memories of bygone love. There is a
touch on my shoulder - a knock at my door - yet no one
is there. I breathe the fragrance of jasmine, though
there be no flowers. Someone calls me - someone
looks at me - an old dream possesses me and leads me
on.

Am Sonntag Morgen (On Sunday morning)   Brahms
I know where you went, so beautifully dressed, on Sunday
morning. Many people who saw you came to tell me.
While they were telling me, I laughed, but that night in
my room, I wept.

An die Nachtigall (To the nightingale)   Brahms
O nightingale, do not sing so loudly your song of love.
Your sweet voice awakens a languishing in my heart. I
am sleepless and look with wet eyes toward the sky. Fly,
nightingale, to the woodland where your mate awaits your
kisses. Fly to her!

An eine Aeolsharfe (To an aeolian harp)   Brahms
The wind which resounds through my aeolian harp comes
from afar and brings the yearning of my beloved one.
In sweet alarm I feel my own longing. Stirred by the
delicate breeze which sings in the aeolian harp, the full
blown rose scatters its petals at my feet.

19

Auf dem Kirchhofe (In the cemetery)   Brahms
On a rainy and stormy day, I wandered among long-
forgotten graves. The names were overgrown and half
legible. On each was the sad word: Deceased. Yet,
how free from all storms they rest. Over every grave
is perfect peace: Released.

Bei dir sind meine Gedanken (My thoughts are with you)
Brahms
My thoughts are with you. They say that you have be-
witched them, and the fire of your eyes has singed their
wings.

Botschaft (Message)   Brahms
Blow, little breeze, gently and sweetly around the cheeks
of my beloved; play tenderly among her curls: do not
fly away hurriedly! If she inquires how I am faring,
tell her: "Endless was his sorrow, and most serious his
plight. But now he can hope to joyfully live again, for
you, lovely one, think of him."

Da unten im Tale (Down there in the valley)   Brahms
Down in the valley, dark waters run, and I cannot tell
you how dearly I love you. You always speak of love
and faithfulness, but there is always some falsehood in
what you say. If I tell you ten times: I love you, and
you do not understand, then I must go on my way. I
thank you for the time when you loved me, but hope you
will do better elsewhere.

Das Mädchen spricht (The maiden speaks)   Brahms
Swallow, tell me, is it with your husband of many years
that you build your nest, or did you only recently marry?
Tell me, what are you whispering in the morning? Are
you a new bride?

Dein blaues Auge (Your blue eye)   Brahms
Your blue eye has so quiet a gaze that I see your very
soul. You ask what I look for there? I see myself
restored. A glowing pair once burned me deep; the
memory pains me still; but yours are clear and cool
as a lake

Der Gang zum Liebchen (Going to the beloved)   Brahms
My dear one keeps her vigil, sighing and weeping as if
she would never again see her lover. I'll hasten and
watch o'er my love. Ye cooing doves, and gentle
breezes, see that no one steals her away.

Der Jäger (The hunter)   Brahms
Oh hunter, what do you seek here by the brook? There
is nothing here to hunt. If you would please my sweetheart, go and shoot the wild boars which break into her
garden, you heroic hunter!

Der Kranz (The wreath)   Brahms
"Mother, help me. Look at this wreath of roses. A
boy made it and asked me to wear it." "Don't be
frightened, daughter, just take the wreath out of your
hair and forget the boy." "But the wreath has thorns,
Mother, that seem to cling to my hair. And the boy
spoke words, Mother, which can never, never be forgotten."

Der Schmied (The blacksmith)   Brahms
When my lover swings his sledge on the anvil there is
the sound of church bells which penetrates the distance.
When I go by, the bellows blow and the flames blaze.

Der Tod das ist die kühle Nacht (Death is the cool night)
Brahms
Death is the cool night and life, the sultry day. The
willows weep where I rest; a nightingale, among the
leaves is singing of love's delight. I hear it though I
be asleep; it haunts my dream.

Die Mainacht (The May night)   Brahms
The nightingale sings in the moonlight of a night in May.
Over my head I hear turtle doves cooing of love, but I
turn away searching for darker shadows. When shall I
look upon the fair and radiant face of my love? The
tears are burning on my cheeks.

Die Sonne scheint nicht mehr (The sun shines no more)
Brahms
The sun shines no more nor sends its cheery light. The
dark and dreary day fades to joyless night. The fire
turns to ashes, yet love is ever burning. O that I were
thine, for no matter what befalls me, the sun would shine
again.

Dort in den Weiden (There in the pasture)   Brahms
A maiden looks out of a window of a house that stands in
a pasture. "Has not the handsomest lad on the Rhine
come?" Each morning he goes down the river and sings
to his bride. "When the glowworm flies and the nightingale sings, I will have my sweetheart with me."

Ein Sonnett (A sonnet)   Brahms
   Ah, if I could only forget her beautiful, lovely being -
   her glance and her enticing lips - I might recover.   But
   my heart cannot forget; yet it is madness to set my
   hopes on her! To linger around her gives courage and
   life - to go away? - never.

Es träumte mir (I dreamed)   Brahms
   I dreamed that I was dear to you, but even as I was
   dreaming, I knew it was a dream.

Feinsliebchen (Dear sweetheart)   Brahms
   My darling, you will never go barefooted. If you will be
   mine, I'll buy you shoes and beautiful dresses.   Though
   you are poor, you have a true and honest will, truth and
   faith that are better than gold.   Here, gentle bride that
   I've loved of old, here, is my ring for you.

Feldeinsamkeit (Solitude in the fields)   Brahms
   I lie still in the tall, green grass, and slowly send my
   glance upward, surrounded by the crickets' incessant
   song, and wrapped in the blue of the heavens.

   The beautiful, white clouds move through the deep blue
   sky like beautiful, quiet dreams; it is as though I have
   been long dead and am travelling joyously with them
   through eternal space.

Geheimnis (Secrecy)   Brahms
   O dusk of spring!   O warm and gentle breezes! Speak,
   you blossoming branches, what are you doing so close together? Are you confiding in one another our secret?
   What are you whispering among yourselves?   About our
   sweet love?

Immer leiser wird mein Schlummer (Ever fainter grows my
slumber)   Brahms
   Ever fainter grows my slumber and sorrow lies veil-like
   over me.   Oft in dreams I hear you calling outside my
   door, but it does not open unto you.   I awake and weep
   bitterly.   Yes, I shall have to die; you will be kissing
   another when I am pale and cold.   If you wish to see me
   again before the May breezes blow, before the thrush
   sings in the wood, come, o come soon.

In dem Schatten meiner Locken (In the shadow of my tresses)
Brahms
   In the shadow of my tresses, my loved one lies asleep.
   Shall I wake my love? Ah, no! With care, I combed my

22

curling tresses in the morning, but all my trouble was
in vain, for the wind soon entangled them again. Tresses
blown by soft winds, have lulled my loved one to sleep.
Shall I wake my love? Ah, no! He must tell me that
his grief is past enduring, that my brown cheeks give
and take life. "Vixen" he has called me - yet he falls
asleep in my presence. Shall I wake him? No!

In der Fremde (Away from home)   Brahms
From my homeland behind the red lightning, clouds come
to me. My father and mother are long since dead; I
have no more friends to see. How soon, how soon,
comes the quiet time in which I, too, shall rest. The
lonely woods envelop me. No one knows me here.

In stiller Nacht (In the still of night)   Brahms
In the still of night, at the first watch, a voice com-
plains. The strong wind brings me the sound of sorrow
and pain, and my heart breaks. The lovely moon longs
to go down and shine no more on sorrow. The stars
long to weep with me. No bird sings any more; I hear
the wild beasts in stony caverns mourning with me.

In Waldeseinsamkeit (Forest solitude)   Brahms
I was sitting at your feet, in forest solitude, and laid
my head on your lap. The sun sank - far off chanted
a nightingale.

Kein Haus, keine Heimat (No house, no hamlet)   Brahms
No house, no hamlet, no wife, no child - so I wander,
a straw in the wind! Tossed out and back, soon there
and soon here; back and forth, and there and here.
World, do not ask of me what I do not ask of thee.

Liebestreu (True love) A dialogue between a mother and her
daughter   Brahms
O sink your sorrow into the deep sea, my child. "A
stone stays on the floor of the sea, but my sorrow always rises to the surface." And the love in your heart,
pluck it out, my child. "A flower dies when one picks
it, but true love does not die so quickly." And your faith,
it is only a word, fling it to the wind. "O mother, even
though the wind might break a rock, my faith can with-
stand it."

Mädchenlied (Maiden song)   Brahms
In the evening the girls spin and sing and laugh with the
boys. It won't be long before the wedding bells will ring
for them. But I am all alone and there is no one to

whom I can open my heart. Tears run down my face - for what am I spinning? I do not know!

Mei Mueter mag mi net (My mother loves me not)   Brahms
"My mother loves me not and I have no lover; sad and dreary is my fate. What good am I? You know that I was not at the fair last Friday because I cannot bear dancing. I want to die." Leave the roses at the cross which you see over her.

Meine Liebe ist grün (My love is green)   Brahms
My love is green as the lilac bush and beautiful as the sun which fills it with fragrance and joy. My soul has nightingale's wings and, drunk with the fragrance of the blooming lilac, it rejoices and sings of love.

Mein Mädel hat einen Rosenmund (My maiden has a rosebud mouth)   Brahms
My sweetheart has a rosebud mouth, and he who kisses it is blest indeed.

Minnelied (Lovesong)   Brahms
The songs of the birds are sweeter when my loved one wanders through the meadows. The lawns become more verdant when her fingers pick the flowers of May. Without her, all is dead, the flowers faded, and the sunset without its splendor. Beloved, never leave me, that my heart may forever bloom with joy.

Nachtigall (Nightingale)   Brahms
Oh nightingale, your plaintive song moves my heart. No, what gives me sweet pain, comes from other, long silenced sounds, which are echoing in your chant.

Nicht mehr zu dir zu gehen (Not to go to you any more) Brahms
I resolved not to go to you any more, and I go every evening: I have no more command over myself, I no longer want to live. I want to die this moment; yet I wish to live for you, with you, and never die. O speak one word only, one single, clear word to give me either life or death; only tell me your true feelings.

Och, Moder, ich well en Ding han! (Oh, mother, I want something!)   Brahms
A girl tells her mother she must have something. "Is it a doll, a new coat, a beautiful ring?" "No." "Is it a husband?" "Yes, Mother, that is what I want!"

O kühler Wald (O cool forest)   Brahms
Where are you, cool forest, in which my beloved walks?
Where are you hiding, o echo, which understands my
song? The forest, in which my beloved walks, rustles
in my heart. The echo sleeps in sorrow - the songs
have wafted away.

O liebliche Wangen (O lovely cheeks)   Brahms
O lovely cheeks, to touch you, and to kiss you fills me
with yearning. My sunlight, o eyes that find and bind
me, you are my joy and the beginning of heaven.   O
heaven on earth, will you be mine? Oh most beautiful
of the beautiful, come quickly, do not delay, show me
that you care, most beautiful one.

O wüsst ich doch den Weg zurück (O would I know the way
back)   Brahms
O would I know the beloved way back to children's land.
Why did I seek for happiness and leave mother's hand?
O how I long to rest, not to be awakened by ambitions,
to close the tired eyes, gently protected by love! And
nothing to seek, nothing to look for, only to gently dream,
not to see the changes of time, to be a child again.   O
would I know the beloved way back to children's land!
In vain I searched for happiness, but all around is emptiness.

Sandmännchen (The little sandman)   Brahms
The little flowers are sleeping beneath the moonbeams,
their heads nodding. The trees sway and sigh as in a
dream, and the little birds, that sang in the sunshine,
are now gone to slumber. The sandman comes through
the window and, should any child not be asleep, sprinkles
sand in its eyes. In the morning, the little eyes will
shine brightly.

Sapphische Ode (Sapphic Ode)   Brahms
I gathered roses at night, they smelled sweeter than in
daytime; dewdrops from the branches touched my hands.
Never did I enjoy the perfume of thy kisses more than
at night, and as from the rose branches, teardrops were
falling down thy cheeks.

Schön war, das ich dir weihte (It was beautiful, what I gave
thee)   Brahms
The golden jewel, I gave thee, was beautiful - and sweet
was the lute's music I played. The heart with which I
gave both was good enough to receive a better reward.

Schwesterlein (Sister dear)   Brahms
"Sister dear, when will we go home?" "Tomorrow when
the cock crows, we will go home." "Sister dear, when
will we go home?" "Tomorrow when the day breaks,
tonight I want my joy." "Sister dear, it is time we left."
"I am dancing with my love, should I leave now, he
would dance with another." "Sister dear, whi are you
so pale?" "That is the morning light on my cheeks."
"Sister dear, you are faint and weak." "Take me to
my little bed, it will be well under the sod."

Sehnsucht (Longing)   Brahms
Behind thick forests - far, far away - is my beloved!
Crumble, mountains! Valleys, level yourselves so that
I may behold my beloved again!

Sonntag (Sunday)   Brahms
A whole week has passed since I saw my sweetheart,
standing at the door, last Sunday. That beautiful maiden
- if only God willed, I were with her today!

Ständchen (Serenade)   Brahms
The moon hangs over the mountain, just right for lovers;
in the garden murmurs a fountain. In yonder arch in
the shadow stand three students with flute, fiddle and
zither, singing and playing. The music enters the dreams
of the sleeping girl who whispers, "Forget-me-not."

Therese   Brahms
Young man, what questions do you ask me in your eyes?
All the wise men would be dumb at your questions.
There is a sea shell at my cousin's drawer; hold it
to your ear, then you will hear something.

Unüberwindlich (Invincible)   Brahms
A thousand times I've sworn not to trust this bottle, yet
I feel newborn when my bartender lets me look upon it
from afar. All hail to you, crystal glass and purple
wine! When the stopper is pulled out, you become empty
and I am not myself! I've sworn a thousand times, also, not to trust this false one, and yet, I feel newborn
when I look into her eyes. Let it be with me as it was
with the strongest man - thy scissors in my hair, ever-
lovely Delila!

Vergebliches Ständchen (The vain courtship)   Brahms
He: Good evening, my sweet! Love brings me to you; please
     open your door!
She:My door is closed, I'll not let you in; my mother told

26

me all is over with me, if I let you in!
He: The night is cold and the wind icy; my heart will freeze
- my love will die. Open the door!
She:If your love dies so easy - let it die! Go home to bed
and sleep. Good night, my boy!

Verrat (Betrayal)   Brahms
I stood, upon a summer night, before my love's house
and heard the door softly grating as she bid another man
farewell. 'I love you - don't keep me waiting,' she said,
'my lover is far away...' 'Leave off love-making, thief!
A man awaits you. You wear a sword - your wooing
shall have my blessing.' At dawn, a dead man lay among
the flowers, to a false maiden's sorrow.''

Vier Ernste Gesänge (Four Serious Songs)   Brahms
1. Denn es gehet dem Menschen, wie dem Vieh (Man is like
the beast)
Death befalleth both the beasts and the sons of man.
Man is not above the beast. Therefore, I perceive
there is no better thing than that a man rejoice in
his own works. That is his lot.

2. Ich wandte mich (I turned around)
I saw all the oppressions beneath the sun. There was
weeping and wailing, and there was no one to comfort
them because their oppressors had power. Then I
praised the dead more than the living, and those not yet
born, because neither of them know the sin done under
the sun.

3. O Tod, wie bitter bist du (O Death, how bitter are you)
O death, how bitter you are to the healthy and those who
have joy. How sweet you are to those who are in want,
ill health, and have nothing to hope for.

4. Wenn ich mit Menschen-oder Engelszungen redete (Though
I speak with the tongues of men)
Though I speak with the tongues of men or of angels,
and have not love, then I am become as sounding brass.
Though I have prophesy and understand all mysteries,
and have not love, I am nothing. And now abideth faith,
hope, love, these three; but the greatest of these is
love.

Von ewiger Liebe (Of eternal love)   Brahms
In the sombre twilight, two lovers are wandering home.
'If you are unhappy and ashamed, our love shall be as

27

quickly ended as begun." The maiden answers. "Our
love shall never fail. It is stronger than iron and steel,
for love is eternal."

Vor dem Fenster (At the window) Brahms
'If the moon shines no brighter, I will go wooing tonight
as I have done before." In the street he sang so beautifully that his beloved leapt out of bed. "Stand still, my
love, do not move or you will wake father and mother,
who do not wish us well. Before your window I must
stand and look at my beautiful love." There the two
stood until the watchman blew his little horn. "O, parting hurts my young heart so much, and I miss my beautiful sweetheart, whom I cannot forget."

Wie bist du meine Königin (How are you, my Queen) Brahms
How beautiful you are, my queen. When you smile, spring
perfumes the air. No rose with you can compare. When
you walk through desert sands, green shadows are spread
to cool it. Let me die within thine arms, for there
death is full of joy.

Wiegenlied (Lullaby) Brahms
Lullaby and good night! If God will, you shall wake
when the morning breaks. Bright angels are near, so
sleep without fear.

Wie Melodien zieht es mir (Like melodies through the soul)
Brahms
Like melodies, it goes lightly through the soul; like
spring flowers, it blows a fragrance hither. Should
words attempt to capture it, it vanishes like a grey mist
and disappears like breath. And yet a fragrance rests
in forgotten rhyme that brings a tear to the eyes.

Wir wandelten (We walked together) Brahms
We walked together, the two of us, and we were both
silent. I would give much to know the unspoken thoughts
that were thine.

Le furet du bois joli (The ferret in the beautiful forest)
Breville
The ferret runs through the trees, awakening dreams of
happiness and evanescent pleasure. Beautiful ladies, do
not try to catch him with your charming lures; in his
struggle he will cruelly snap at you and cause you tears.
Flee from him. The happiness this villain brings is
fleeting and ends sadly.

Cara, si, tu mi consumi (Beloved, yes, you destroy me)
Buononcini
Beloved, yes, you destroy me. You make me suffer
though my heart beats only for you. Your eyes have the
power to make the forests, the rivers, and even the
stones, fall in love with you.

L'esperto nocchiero   Buononcini
Why does the wise sailor change his course after leaving
in the morning? Wild winds have arisen, and he returns to the shelter of the harbor before he is wrecked
by the gale.

Per la gloria d'adorarvi (I adore and love you) Buononcini
I adore and love you, bright eyes, even though love
brings me suffering. Without hope for joy, affection and
sighing are futile. But who can look at your sweet light
and not love you?

Amarilli   Caccini
Believe without doubting, but should fear beset you, open
my heart and you'll see written in it, "Amarilli is my
love."

Tu ch'ai le penne, Amore (You, who has wings, Cupid)
Caccini
You, Cupid, spread your wings and fly to my beloved.
If you do not know the road, just follow my sighs. Go
'til you find my love: her white breasts are covered
with a veil and her eyes have luminous rays.

Alma del core   (Soul of the heart)   Caldara
Soul of the heart, breath of my very spirit, I'll faithfully
adore thee forever. I'll gladly languish in all my anguish
if I may kiss those red lips once more.

Come raggio di sol (As sunbeams)   Caldara
As sunbeams are resting upon the waves, while in the
ocean's bosom the storm awakes, so are red lips smiling,
gay and content, while the wounded heart trembles and
suffers.

Sebben, crudele (Although, you cruel one)   Caldara
Although, you cruel one, make me love-sick, I shall love
you forever!

Selve amiche (Friendly woods)   Caldara
Friendly woods, shadowy plants, faithful haven of my
heart. You will give this loving soul peace from suffering.

Granadinas   Calleia
Farewell! My Granada. I will see you nevermore.
My heart is filled with great sorrow to go so far from
your sight, and to leave my beloved Morenita.

Le papillon (The butterfly), from "Les Fêtes Vénitiennes"
Campra
Charming butterfly, whose golden wings drift through the
air like petals, would that I could fly away with you!

Chants d'Auvergne (Excerpts)   Canteloube
1. Berceus (Lullaby)
Sleep, descend quickly; sleep, come here. But it
doesn't want to come. The child doesn't want to sleep.
Oh, come, sleep, descend. It arrives, it is here. The
poor little one wants to sleep.

2. Malheureux qui a une femme (Unhappy is he who has
a woman)
Unhappy is he who has a woman. Unhappy is he who
doesn't have one. He who hasn't one, wants one. He
who has one, doesn't want her. Happy is the woman
who has a man who pleases her. But happer still is
she who doesn't have one.

3. Viens par le pré (Come into the meadow)
Come into the meadow, my beautiful; I shall go by the
forest. When you are there, you will come with me, if
you wish. We shall speak, darling, together. It is
your love which makes me happy.

O sole mio (Oh, my sunshine) Capua
What better thing is there than sunshine following the
storm? The sunshine in your eyes!

Vittoria, mio core (Victorious my heart) Carissimi
My heart is victorious and there will be no more tears,
for the shackles of love have been broken. The false
one is now gone; her glances can no longer deceive me
- they only amuse me. The cruel flame of love is now
spent. Victorious is my heart!

Apemantus's grace   Castelnuovo-Tedesco
At the great banquet in Timon's house appears Apemantus,
churlist philosopher, who scorns the rich foods and
wines, accepting only a drink of "honest water, which
ne'er left man i' the mire" - for which he offers his own
peculiar grace.

La capella di San Simon (The chapel of San Simon)
Castelnuovo-Tedesco
   To the chapel of San Simon in Seville, all the ladies go
   to pray. My lady, the most beautiful, gorgeously
   dressed and with lipstick and rouge, upon entering the
   chapel puts a drop of alcohol in her eyes to make them
   sparkle. The little abbott who says mass is unable to
   recite. The little novices who help him do not know
   what to reply, and instead of saying "Amen," they say
   "Amour."

The soldier drinks   Castelnuovo-Tedesco
   In the great hall of the palace, Iago, reveling with soldiers there, sings a lusty song for their entertainment.

Ebben? ne andò lontana (I go far away), from "La Wally"
Catalani
   And now? I shall go as the echo of the pious bell, towards
   the white snow - towards the golden clouds, where hope
   is sorrow and grief. From my mother's friendly house
   I shall go, never to see it again, never to return.

Donzelle, fugite (Maiden, flee)   Cavalli
   Maiden, pay less respect to outward beauty! If a bright
   glance penetrates your heart, flee that arrow of frivolous
   love which may wound you!

Intorno all' idol mio (Around my idol)   Cesti
   Around my idol breathe lightly, soothing and sprightly
   Zephyrs. Breezes, carry my sweet kisses to his cheek.
   Carry tender dreams to him who has surrendered his
   spirit to restful night. May his dreams reveal all my
   passion and my longing.

Villanelle des petits canards (Country song of the ducks)
Chabrier
   They waddle, the little ducks, just like the good country
   folk. Marching along, each about his own affairs -
   chattering like firecrackers - making love through their
   noses - they waddle, just like the good country folk.

Depuis le jour (Since the day), from "Louise"   Charpentier
   Since the day I gave myself to thee, my life is beautiful
   like a flowergarden. Thy first kiss intoxicated my soul!
   What a beautiful life - I am so happy! I see only
   laughter, light and joy! I tremble with delight when
   thinking of our first day of love! I am so happy!

CHAUSSON

Chausson, a man of wealth and of serene and meditative nature, was a student of Franck. His songs are gracious and gently lyrical, of a sensitive nature, and frequently of a melancholy mood. Of his 35 songs, few are in the concert repertoire of today. Those which are most frequently sung are rich in color and modulation, possessing an unusual affinity with the poetic line.

Le colibri (The humming-bird)   Chausson

The green humming-bird, at morning, flies like a breeze into the air. He wings his way to the sweet hibiscus and drinks so much from its rosy cup that he dies. On your beloved lips, my soul, likewise, would drink the perfume of our first kiss.

Les papillons (The butterflies)   Chausson

The butterflies, snowy and fleecy, fly in cloudy swarms o'er the sea; happy butterflies, were your easy flight in the azure but for me!

Poeme De L'Amour Et De La Mer (Poem of love and of the sea)   Chausson

1.   La fleur des eaux.   (The water flower)
The air is filled with an exquisite perfume of lilacs.
The sea, in the heat of the sun, is all aflame. Over the fine sands, which they kiss, roll the sparkling waves.
My heart is awakened on this summer morn, for you, a lovely child, stood on the shore, gazing at me. My heart flew toward you. You took it and held it.

How doleful and wild a sound. The sea rolls along the shore, mocking and caring not that this is the hour of parting. My very soul has been taken from me, and the somber roar of the waves covers the sound of my sobs. Who knows whether this cruel sea will bring her back to my heart? The sea sings, and the mocking wind jeers at my heart's anguish.

2.   La mort de l'amour (The death of love)
Soon, that blue and joyful island will appear to me, among the rocks. Across the amethyst sea, the boat softly glides. I shall be both happy and sad, remembering so much, so soon. My thoughts are tossed about like the dead leaves dancing in the night wind; the leaves seem to sigh, and to speak of the inexpressible horror of love that is dead. My blood froze when I saw my beloved so strangely smiling; like the faces of the dead, our faces had paled. Speechless, bending over her, I could read this fatal word

written in her eyes: oblivion.

3. Les temps des lilas (The time of lilacs)
    The time of lilacs and time of roses will not come back
    again; the time of lilacs and the time of roses has
    passed; and gone are the carnations too. The wind has
    changed, the skies are somber, and we shall never again
    hasten to gather the blooming lilacs and the lovely roses;
    the spring is sad and cannot flourish. Oh joyful and
    sweet season of the year, which came to steep us in its
    sunlight, our flower of love has faded so much that your
    kiss cannot wake it again! No more budding flowers,
    no more gay sunshine nor cooling shades; the time of
    lilacs and the time of roses, with our love, is dead for-
    ever.

Lamento di Federico (Federico's lament), from "L'Arlesiana"
Cilea
    The delightfully melodious score of "L'Arlesiana" sup-
    ports the simple story of love, jealousy, and death.
    Federico, enamored by the beautiful peasant girl from
    Arles, finds her in the arms of a rival and chooses to
    die rather than live without her love. -- "O that I could
    forget all, and have peace of mind like the shepherd boy.
    Alas, all efforts are in vain;... Her beautiful image is
    before me always. Why must I endure so much pain?
    O, fatal vision, leave me!"

Fiocca la neve (The snow is falling)   Cimara
    "It is snowing," while written by a modern composer, is
    not in the modern idiom; rather it is in the bel canto
    style which stresses melodic beauty. The words are by
    G. Pascoli. "White flakes of snow come flitting down," an
    aged woman in a squalid home sits, singing to a baby,
    telling him that his couch is like a garden bower.

The statue of Czarskoe-Selo   Cui
    The urn is broken on the rock when the maiden bends
    o'er for water. Sadly her tears flow o'er the forlorn
    fragments.
    Suddenly, an unbelievable miracle occurs! A sparkling
    fountain gushes from the urn.
    Yet, o'er the ripples, she weeps eternally.

La coeur de ma mie (The heart of my sweetheart) Dalcroze
    My beloved's heart is quite tiny, and is filled with love
    for me. If her heart were not so small, there would be

room in it for more than one sweetheart. My heart is larger than hers, but if it were in a still larger body, it would hold love for her alone.

DEBUSSY

Debussy, a friend of many of the artists of his time, has been called the great impressionist. His music was a revolt against musical extravagance and a reaction to the heavy romanticism typified by Wagner and his followers. Tempered in dynamics, his songs have a vivid color of harmony associated with a frequent use of the whole tone scale. He found great inspiration in French poets, and in his settings of their lyrics, the association of word and music is so close that one must understand the beauties of the one to understand the other. His forty-seven songs were written during all periods of his life and are characterized by an ethereal quality, both mystic and sensual.

Air de Lia, from "L'Enfant Prodigue" Debussy
Year after year passes in vain! Seasons, games and diversions sadden me: they reopen my wound and my sorrow deepens... Lia ever laments the child she has no more!... Azaël! Why have you forsaken me?...How calm the evenings were, when the toil was over and all people praised the blessed hand of the Lord. Others do not feel the weight of old age. Finding happiness in their children, they watch the years pass by without regret and without sadness. In disconsolate hearts, time weighs heavily! Azaël, why have you forsaken me?

Ariettes Oubliées Debussy
1. C'est l'extase (This is ecstasy)
This is languorous ecstasy, with the rustling of forests in the embrace of the breeze. This is the chorus of little voices. The soul which is lamenting in this subdued plaint is ours, is it not? Say that it is mine and yours which breathes this humble hymn on this mild evening.

2. Il pleure dans mon coeur (Tears fall in my heart)
Tears fall in my heart like the rain upon the city. Tears fall without reason in my anguished heart. This mourning has no reason. It is truly the keenest pain not to know why, without either love or hate, my heart bears so much pain.

3. L'ombre des arbres (The shadow of the trees)
The reflections of the trees in the river are vanishing

like smoke, while in the air, the turtle doves lament.
How much this pallid landscape mirrors your own pale
self, and how sadly weep your drowned hopes!

4. Chevaux de bois (Wooden horses)
   Whirl around, good wooden horses! A hundred turns -
   a thousand turns! Go and never stop - turn around to
   the tune of the oboes. Turn around, hobby horses, without ever needing the aid of spurs to make you gallop.
   Turn - without hope of any hay.

5. Green (Green)
   Here are fruits, flowers, leaves and branches, and here
   is my heart, which beats only for you. Do not tear it
   apart with your white hands. On your young bosom, let
   me cradle my head, still filled with music from your
   last kisses. Let it be soothed, and let me sleep a little,
   while you rest.

6. Spleen (Spleen)
   Beloved, when you are a little restless, all my despair
   is reborn. I am always afraid of what may come, of
   some cruel flight of yours! I am weary of everything
   except you. Alas!

Azaël's Recitative and Aria, from "L'Enfant Prodigue" Debussy
   These happy tunes oppress my heart and trouble my
   mind. Here, under the swaying branches, I watch my
   brother and my sister. They are happy! Oh, days gone
   by, when this serene nature gave strength to my tired
   body and when, overjoyed to press my head upon mother's
   heart, I knew nothing of life but innocence and happiness! Why has my soul forced me to forsake that place?
   ...Throughout the night I slowly cross the perilous
   paths...

Beau soir (Beautiful evening)   Debussy
   When, in the setting sun, the streams are rosy, and when
   a warm breeze floats over the fields of grain, a counsel
   to be happy seems to emanate from all things and rise
   toward the troubled heart. It is an advice to enjoy the
   pleasure of being alive, while one is young and the evening is beautiful; for we shall go as this wave goes - it,
   to the sea - we, to the grave.

Chansons De Bilitis   Debussy
1. La flûte de Pan (The flute of Pan)
   For the day of Hyacinthus, he gave me a pipe made of
   well-cut reeds, joined with white wax - sweet as honey

35

on my lips. He teaches me to play, while I sit trembling on his knees. He plays so soft - I hardly hear him. Our songs harmonize and gradually our lips are united on the flute. It is late - mother will never believe that I stayed out so long in search of my lost belt.

2. La chevelure (Her hair)
He said to me, "This night I dreamed I was feeling your hair around my neck and upon my bosom. I caressed your hair - it was my own. And we are united forever by our tresses, with lips upon lips." When he ceased to speak, he gently placed his hands upon my shoulders, and he looked at me so tenderly that with a sudden thrill I lowered my eyes.

3. Le tombeau des Naïades (The tomb of the Naïads)
I wandered along the frost-covered woods, my hair with tiny icicles, my sandals heavy with packed snow. He asked me: "What are you looking for?" I follow the trace of Satyr. He told me: "The Satyrs are dead and also the Nymphs. The hoofprint which you see is that of a buck. But let us stay here, on the site of their tomb." And with the iron of his hatchet, he broke through the ice of the spring where the Naïads once had laughed. He peered through large frozen pieces, holding them toward the sky.

Cinq Poèmes De Baudelaire   Debussy
1. Le balcon (The balcony)
Mother of memory, mistress of mistresses, you are all my pleasure and have all of my esteem. You will recall the beauty of caresses, the evenings illumined by the glow of coals, and the rose perfumed moments on the balcony. I know the art of evoking happy moments. Were those vows, those perfumes, and those endless kisses reborn out of a depth beyond our reach, like the sun rises to the sky after it has bathed at the bottom of deep oceans?

2. Harmonie du soir (Evening harmony)
Now comes the time when each flower exhales fragrance like a censer; the violin vibrates like a heart in distress, a melancholy waltz and a languorous intoxication fills the air, the sky is sad and beautiful, like a great altar, the sun has drowned in its own blood. A tender heart recalls all memories of the luminous past. My memory of you shines like a monstrance.

3. Le jet d'eau (The fountain)

Your beautiful eyes are weary, my beloved! Rest a
while, without opening them, in this carefree pose in
which pleasure has come upon you. In the courtyard the
fountain chatters day and night, sustaining sweetly the
ecstasy in which love has engulfed me tonight. The
column of water, which the moon penetrates with its pale
light, falls like a shower of large tears. So your soul,
setting aflame the fiery lightning of desire, leaps quickly
toward the vast, enchanted skies. Then it diffuses, dying in a wave of sad languor which, by way of an invisible incline, descends to the depths of my heart. Oh, I
find it sweet, leaning against your bosom, to listen to
the eternal lament that sobs in the fountain.

4. Recueillement (Introspection)
   Be wise, my sorrow, and more calm; you wanted the
   evening - it is here! A dark haze envelopes the city,
   bringing to some peace, to others anxiety. While the
   multitude of mortals, under the whip of pleasure, will
   suffer the pangs of remorse at the lowly feast, sorrow
   of mine, give me your hand, come hither, far away from
   them. And like a long shroud trailing towards the East,
   hear, beloved, the gentle night approaching.

5. La mort des amants (The death of lovers)
   We shall have beds scented with faint perfumes, and
   strange flowers on the shelves unfolding for us beneath
   the most beautiful skies; our two hearts will be two
   great torches, reflecting their double light in our two
   spirits, these twin mirrors. On an evening spun of rose
   and mystic blue, we shall exchange a single lightning
   flash, like a long sob charged with parting, and later,
   an angel will restore to life, faithful and joyful, the
   tarnished mirrors and the extinct flames.

Dans le jardin (In the garden)   Debussy
   In the garden I looked furtively across the hedge and saw
   you, child. My heart trembled in love. My fingers bled
   from the scratches of thorns; my suffering was divine.
   I saw your face, your golden hair, blue eyes, and charming body; your voice was of May and gave gestures of
   April. I loved you!

Fêtes Galantes   Debussy
1. En sourdine (Muted)
   Serene in the twilight made by the branches, let our love
   be imbued with this deep silence. And when the night
   will fall from the black oaks, voice of our despair, the
   nightingale shall sing.

2. Clair de lune (Moonlight)
Your soul is like a landscape where charming masqueraders are playing the lute and dancing, almost sad beneath their fantastic disguises, while singing, in a soft
way, of triumphant love and a pleasant life. They do not
believe in their happiness. Their song, blending with the
moonlight, lulls the birds in the trees to sleep and makes
the fountains sob with ecstasy.

3. Fantoches (Phantoms)
Scaramouche and Pulcinella, brought together by wicked
intentions, gesture in the faint moonlight as Doctor Bo-
lonais gathers herbs. His pretty daughter roguishly
slips, semi-nude, under the hawthorn bush in search of
her handsome Spanish pirate. A nightingale sings in distress.

Fleur de blés (Flower of the grainfield)   Debussy
Beside the grainfields, I gathered a bouquet for you. It
is fashioned in your likeness, this golden grain is the
wave of your blonde hair, this swaying poppy is the
blood-red of your lips, and these cornflowers are your
eyes - two lightning flashes descended from the sky.

La belle au bois dormant (Sleeping beauty)   Debussy
A knight passes at dusk, his hair under a moon-colored
helmet. Sleep in the wood, o Beauty, with the ring on
your finger. He has killed loyally and justly, as a king
would fight. Astride his great charger, he races breathlessly, bolt upright in his stirrups. Sleep, Beauty, and
dream that a prince will wed you. But he has taken the
ruby ring, the knight with hair bright as sunshine. Sleep
no longer, Beauty, the ring is no longer on your finger.

La grotte (The grotto)   Debussy
Near this dark grotto, where one inhales a soft air, the
wave battles with the stones and the light with the shade.
The floods, tired from their journey over the gravel,
rest in this grotto, where time ago Narcissus died. The
ghosts of this rosy flower, and of the constant rushes,
appear to be in the dreams of the slumbering water.

La mer est plus belle (The sea is more beautiful)   Debussy
The sea, over which prays the Virgin Mary, is more
beautiful than the cathedrals. It is a faithful nurse,
soothing the rattle of death. It has all qualities, terrible
and gentle, forgiving and angry. A friendly breeze
haunts the wave and sings to us: "You, without hope,
may die without suffering!"

L'echelonnement des haies (The row of hedges)   Debussy
The row of hedges winds unendingly, a sea distinct in
the transparent mist, fragrant with young bayberries.
Trees and windmills pose airily atop the soft green,
where gaily romp and cavort the frisky colts. In this
Sunday haze are also playing the large sheep, as soft as
their white fleece. All at once unfurled, the waves roll
on shoals. The bells sound like flutes in the milk-
white sky.

Le faune (The faun)   Debussy
An old faun, wrought in terra cotta, laughs amid the
greensward; forseeing, no doubt, an evil outcome to these
tranquil moments which have led me on, and thou, too -
melancholy pilgrims both - until this hour, whose flight
whirls away to the sound of the tambourines.

Les Angélus (The Angelus)   Debussy
The Christian bells tell the heart not to lose hope! But
today my grief is supreme. I live only in shadow and
night. The tired angelus weeps of death. In my sub-
missive heart sleeps the lonely widow of all hope.

Les cloches (The bells)   Debussy
The leaves opened delicately along the branches. The
bells were ringing beneath the fair sky. The distant
call brought to my mind the whiteness of Altar-flowers.
The bells spoke of happy years, and in the forest, the
faded leaves seemed green again as in days long past.

Mandoline   Debussy
Serenaders and fair listeners chat idly beneath the
whispering branches. Their short silken jackets, their
long trailing gowns, their elegance, their gladness, and
their soft blue shadows whirl in the ecstasy of moonlight,
pink and gray, and the mandoline chatters in the trembling breeze.

Noëls des enfants (Children's Christmas)   Debussy
A Christmas carol for homeless children for which Debussy, the great French impressionist, wrote both the
words and the music. "We no longer have any homes,
the enemy has taken everything. Father is in the war;
Mother is dead. What can we do now? Oh, Noel!
Punish the enemy and avenge the children of France, of
Belgium, of Serbia and of Poland. We do not want toys,
only our daily bread, our shoes, and Victory to the children of France."

Nuit d'étoiles (Night of stars)   Debussy
Night of stars, amid your breezes and your scents, I
dream of my late loves.   Melancholy unfolds in my heart
and I sense the soul of my beloved, trembling in the
forest.   I see again your glances, blue as the sky; the
rose is your breath and the stars are your eyes.

Paysage sentimental (Sentimental landscape)   Debussy
The soft wintry sky, sad and sleepy, resembled the feeling which made us both happy and a little melancholy on
that afternoon of kisses beneath the dark boughs.   Oh,
how tender were your lips in that silent wood and in the
languor of the year's death, - death of everything except
you, my beloved, and except happiness, which overflows
my heart.

Proses Lyriques   Debussy
1.   De rêve (A dream)
The night has the tenderness of a woman, and the old
trees dream in the golden moonlight of the one whose
head was wreathed in pearls and who has vanished.   The
frail and the frenzied, who sowed laughter, have disappeared.   The old trees weep their leaves of gold, gone
forever their golden helmets.   Strange sighs arise from
the trees.   My spirit grasps you in an ancient dream.

2.   De grève (The shore)
The twilight, like veils of white silk, falls over the ocean.
The rustling waves chatter like little girls in their green
iridescent silk.   The waves scatter before the downpour,
but the moonlight caresses her little friends who offer
themselves to the warm, white kiss like loving lips.
Then, nothing more except bells, the Angelus of the
waves and white smooth silk.

3.   De fleurs (Flowers)
In the despair of the greenhouse of sorrow, the evil
stems of flowers entwine about my heart.   Oh, when will
I again feel those tender soothing hands on my head?   My
soul is dying of too much sun - the sun that causes evil
flowers to bloom, and destroys the dreams and illusions
which are the blessed friends of souls in despair.   Joy
will never bloom again, my eyes are weary of weeping
and my hands weary of praying.

4.   De soir (Evening)
Sunday in the towns and in the hearts!   The little girls
are singing gay little tunes.   On Sunday, people say good-
bye and leave for adventure.   On Sunday, my heart

mourns for those Sundays that are gone. The night lulls the lonely, weary sky to sleep and the Virgin, of gold on silver, sows the flowers of slumber. Have pity on the towns and on the hearts, Virgin of gold on silver!

Romance   Debussy
Where have the winds driven the fleeting, suffering, gentle and fragrant soul of the lilies I gathered in the garden of your thoughts? Does no fragrance remain of those blissful days, fashioned of hope, faithful love, and peace?

Trois Ballades de François Villon   Debussy
1. Ballade de Villon à s'amye (Ballade of Villon to his love) Here the disillusioned, bitter poet cries for release from "false loveliness" that costs a heavy price, a love that is hard as rock though it seems "soft and fair."

2. Ballade que Villon fait à la requeste de sa mère pour prier Nostro-Dame (Ballade made at the request of Villon's Mother as a prayer to the Virgin Mary) In this song the poet and the composer capture the humble and devout faith of Villon's mother: "In this faith I wish to live and die."
3. Ballade des femmes de Paris (Ballade of the women of Paris) This song expresses the conviction that no women, of any time, can equal those of Paris for chattering.

Voici que le printemps (Here is spring)   Debussy
Here is Spring, welcomed like a prince upon his return from long exile. He carries a nightingale on his left shoulder and a blackbird on his right. The flowers which slept under the moss awake and listen to the songs of the birds. The blackbird whistles for the unloved, and the nightingale sings a long, languishing and moving song for lovers.

Bell Song, from "Lakmé"   Delibes
The song tells of a low caste maiden, shunned by every-one, who rescues the God Vishnu from the wild beasts. Vishnu carries her to heaven.

Bon jour, Suzon (Good morning, Suzon!)   Delibes
Good morning, Suzon! I'm home again, and you're still the prettiest maiden here. I've made love and verses, far and wide, but you're the one I choose. So let me in your door, I pray. Good morning, Suzon!

Le rossignol (The nightingale)   Delibes
Listen to the nightingale! We sing of love when the soft
night is above or when daylight approaches.   "Love
returns every year," says the shepherd maiden.   "Nay,"
sings the nightingale, "when once it has departed, it is
gone forever.   Sweet love comes but once, alas!"

Les filles de Cadix (The maids of Cadix)   Delibes
In this infectious song of Spain, an atmosphere of castanets and guitars alike pervades the words of Alfred de
Musset and the music of Delibes.   The song itself tells
in two stanzas just what the maids of Cadix will tolerate
in the way of flirtation.   Flatter them discreetly and all
is well.   But let a dashing hidalgo say, "If thou wilt be
mine, speak, and this gold is thine!" and, as the refrain goes, "Such words as these are distasteful to the
maids of Cadix."

O del mio amato ben (Oh my dear beloved)   Donaudy
Oh my dear beloved, gone forever from me, you were my
glory and my pride.   I search through rooms, so
hushed and stilled, and call with throbbing heart.   My
search and call is in vain; my only solace is in weeping.

Spirate pur spirate (Blow gently little breeze)   Donaudy
Blow gently about my dear one, little breeze, that you
may discover whether her heart holds my image.   Now,
blow, o breezes!

Aria of Linda, from "Linda di Chamounix"   Donizetti
Ah! I have arrived too late at our meeting place and
missed my beloved Carlo...and who knows how much he
suffered - but not as much as I.   He left me those beautiful flowers.   The day of our marriage approaches, oh
happiness.
Oh, light of this soul, delight, love and life.   We shall
be together on earth and in heaven.   Oh, come to me,
rest on my heart that sighs, wants you and beats only for
you.

Cercherò lontana terra (I will search in distant lands) "Don
Pasquale"   Donizetti
Victim of a cruel uncle, Ernesto sings sadly of his de-
cision to seek a new life far from his beloved Norina.

Com' è gentil (How gentle), from "Don Pasquale"   Donizetti
How sweet is the Spring night.   The sky is blue and the
moon so clear.   All is languor, peace, mystery and love.

My dear, why don't you come to me? When I am really
dead, you will cry, but you cannot call me back to life.

Duet: Ecco il magico liquore (This is the magic potion),
from "L'Elisir d'Amore" Donizetti
Dulcamara, a quack doctor, appears among the villagers
in his splendid carriage with his trunkful of wonderful
nostrums whose virtues he extols in song. To the love-
sick Nemorino, the doctor is heaven-sent and he immediately asks for some love elixir. Dulcamara is quite
puzzled with this strange request but loses no time in pro-
ducing a bottle of strong wine which he says is the cov-
eted potion.

O mio Fernando (O my Fernando), from "La Favorita"
Donizetti
Is it true, o Fernando, that you are the fair Leonora's
husband? To marry him would bring only a dower of
shame. No, though he curses me, I shall disappear
rather than ask him to pity the outcast who loves him.

Regnava nel silenzio (Silence was reigning), from "Lucia di
Lammermoor" Donizetti
Silence was reigning and the night was dark when the
spectre appeared on yonder fountain. It threatened with
its phantom hand and in a moment vanished away. Suddenly the pure water turned to the color of blood. Soon
the clouds floated away and the moonlight showed nature,
in smiling sleep, robed in splendor.

Una furtive lagrima (A furtive tear), from "L'Elisir d'Amore"
Donizetti
A furtive tear glistened in her eyes, as if she seemed to
envy the festive youngsters. Why do I search further?
She loves me, yes, I am aware of it. Oh could I, for
one moment, feel the beating of her lovely heart, and
join our sighs together. Oh heaven, I could desire no
more and then would gladly die.

DUPARC
Duparc, in later life, destroyed many of his songs, leaving to posterity only fifteen songs which can all be described as masterpieces. A student of Franck, his songs
have a superb musical diction and an intense passion
through large and vibrant musical phrases.

Chanson triste (Sad song) Duparc
In your heart there sleeps a moonlight, a soft moonlight
of summer, and to escape this troublesome life, I shall

forget the past sorrows, my love, when you will cradle
my sad heart and my thoughts in the loving stillness of
your arms! You will let my wounded head, oh, sometimes rest on your knees, and you will recite a ballad,
a ballad that will seem to speak of us, and in your eyes,
filled with sadness, in your eyes then I shall drink so
many kisses and tender caresses that perhaps I shall recover.

Elegie (Elegy)   Duparc
Do not whisper his name! Let him sleep in the shade,
where his remains repose. Silent and sad fall our tears,
like the dew, which make the verdure on his resting
place glitter. Our tears will keep his memory fresh and
green in our hearts.

Extase (Extasy)   Duparc
On a pale blossom my heart sleeps a slumber sweet as
death. Blissful death perfumed by the breath of the beloved. On thy pale bosom my heart sleeps a slumber
sweet as death.

La vie antérieure (The previous life)   Duparc
I have lived by the sea where the sun, piercing through
grottos of clouds, made a picture of majestic columns.
The majestic tide played its mighty chords under the reflected sun of evening. It was there that I lived among
slaves, who cooled my fevered forehead with palm
leaves, and cared for my sorrow.

Lamento (Lament)   Duparc
Do you know the white tomb, where floats the shadow of
a yew-tree, in which a pale dove sings its song? It is
like the awakened soul that weeps under the earth in uni-
son with the song and complaints of having been forgotten.
Never more shall I go near the tomb, when evening descends, to hear the pale dove sing its plaintive song!

Le manoir de Rosemonde (The house of Rosemonde)   Duparc
With a bite deep and cruel has love wounded me. Passing where I have gone, you can follow my trail in blood.
You can see how, lonely and hurt, I roamed this sad world
and came at last to die far away, without ever finding the
blue dwelling of Rosemonde.

L'Invitation au voyage (Invitation to the voyage)   Duparc
My child, my sister, dream of the sweetness of living,
loving and dying together in the land that resembles you
in its splendor. The sunlight of these misty skies is to

me like the charm of your eyes, shining through tears.
Everything there is beauty, luxury, calm and pleasure.

Phidylé   Duparc
The grass is soft for slumbering under the cool poplar
trees by the slope of the mossy springs, which in the
flowering meadows, sprouting in thousands, lose themselves among the dark thickets. Rest, oh Phidylé!
Noonday on the leaves sparkles and invites you to slumber! Among the clover and the thyme, alone in the full
sunshine, the bees hum in their flight; a warm perfume
fills the air at the turn of the paths; the red poppy is
drooping, and the birds, grazing the hill with their wings,
seek the shade of the wild rosebushes. Rest, oh Phidylé! But, when the orb, descending in its brilliant
curve, will cool its smouldering heat, let your loveliest
smile and your tenderest kiss reward me, reward me
for waiting!

Sérénade florentine (Florentine serenade)   Duparc
Star, whose beauty like a diamond illuminates the night,
bring to my beloved as she sleeps, the benediction of the
heavens. Enter her room, and as a kiss, touch her lips
until the coming of dawn that she may dream of a star
of love which rises for her.

Soupir (Sighing)   Duparc
Never to see nor to hear her. Never to call out her
name, but, faithfully, always to wait for her, always to
love her! To open one's arms out, and tired of waiting,
to close them on the void! But yet, always to hold them
out to her. Always to love her. Always!

Mandoline   Dupont
Serenaders and fair listeners chat idly beneath the whispering branches. Their short silken jackets, their long
trailing gowns, their elegance, their gladness, and their
soft blue shadows whirl in the ecstasy of moonlight. The
mandoline chatters in the trembling breeze.

Danza, danza fanciulla (Dance, dance my sweet child)   Durante
Dance, dance, my sweet child, to my singing. Turn
lightly and gracefully to the sound like the waves of the
sea. Do you hear the whispering of the morning-breeze,
which talks to the heart with a languishing sound and invites you to dance?

Vergin, tutta amor (Virgin, full of compassion)   Durante
Virgin, full of compassion. Most holy Mary, hear my

prayer, as tearfully I bow to Thee. May my tears move Thee to hear my lamenting. Mary have pity, assuage my sorrow and grief.

O bellissimi capelli (O beautiful locks)   Falconieri
Locks so beautiful and shining, oh, my sweetest delectation. Into rings and clusters twining for a lover's adoration.

Vezzosette e care (Graceful and dear)   Falconieri
Graceful and dear eyes, with tender and bright glances, why are you so cautious with your radiant splendor?

Villanella (Country-song)   Falconieri
Beautiful young maiden with the rosy cheeks - you have enslaved me. Have pity on your poor servant. Don't let me die!
O! dear young fellow with the laughing eyes which shine with such charming glances. Please bring an end to my great sorrow. Don't let me die!

Siete Canciones Populares Españolas (Seven Spanish folksongs)   Falla
1. El paño moruno (The moorish cloth)
    If that cloth is stained, it will sell for little or nothing.

2. Seguidilla murciana (Murcian seguidilla)
    People who live in glass houses should take this warning: Beware how you throw stones at your neighbors. We are muleteers and shall meet again on our journeys! Because you are so flighty, I will compare you to a penny which has passed from hand to hand until it is worn and looks false. Then nobody will take it.

3. Asturiana
    Looking for consolation, I went to a green pine and upon seeing me weep, it wept too!

4. Jota
    They say we do not love each other because we keep our love for us. If they would test your heart and mine, they would find true love. In sorrow I leave you - it may not please your mother. Farewell, sweetheart.

5. Nana (Lullaby)
    Sleep well, my angel - sleep well, little morning star.

6. Canción (Song)

I want to forget your traitorous eyes. You do not know
what anguish it is to watch them. They say you do not
want me, but I was once your lover.

7. Polo
My sorrow I keep in my heart! Accursed be love and
the one who brought love to me!

FAURÉ
Fauré, besides being a writer of over one hundred songs,
was an organist and teacher, numbering among his students such composers as Enesco, Ravel, Boulanger and
Schmitt. His songs, written over a period of some sixty
years, are models of economy and harmonic inventive-
ness. His knowledge of Gregorian themes, and his great
facility as an improviser on them, seemingly had a profound influence on his melodic line. His songs, all settings of verses of his time, are deceptively simple and
fluent, yet even when light and gay, they tend to be wist-
ful and melancholy.

Après un Rêve (After a dream)   Fauré
In a slumber, charmed by your image, I dreamed of
happiness - ardent mirage. Your eyes were more gentle,
your voice pure and clear. You were radiant like a sky
brightened by sunrise. You called me and I left the
earth to flee with you towards the light. The skies
opened their clouds for us - splendors unknown - glimpses
of divine light. Alas, alas, sad awakening from dreams!
I call to you, oh night, give me back your illusions.
Return, return with your radiance, return, oh mysterious
night!

Aurore   Fauré
From night's gardens the stars are fleeing, golden bees
attracted by invisible honey. In the distance, dawn
spreads the brightness of its curtain, weaves silver
threads into the blue mantle of heaven. From my heart's
garden my desires are fleeing with the awakening of the
morning, like bees to the copper horizon. They fly to
your feet like stars chased by the clouds, exiled from the
golden heaven where your beauty blooms, and seek to
reach you by unknown paths, blending their dying light
with the new born day.

Automne (Autumn)   Fauré
Autumn, with cloudy skies and pale dawns and days filled
with melancholy! My thoughts are carried back on the
wings of regret to those days when I was young, and

wandered in dreams over the enchanted hills. In recalling the past, the forgotten tears of my heart fill my eyes.

Avant que tu ne t'en ailles (Before you fly away)   Fauré
Before you go away, morning star, shine on the poet whose eyes are full of love. Shine in the dawn where my love lies sleeping. Quickly, because there always is the sand of sleep.

Chanson d'amour (Song of love)   Fauré
I love your eyes, I love your brow, Ah! my rebel, my wild one.

Clair de lune (Moonlight)   Fauré
Your soul is a landscape where spirits, like masqueraders, play their lutes when they dance. There is sadness beneath their disguises, for, though they sing of love and life, they seem to doubt that love and life are real. In the moonlight their songs bring tender dreams to the birds and ecstasy to the fountains.

Dans les ruines d'une veille abbaye (In the ruins of an ancient abbey)   Fauré
Two newly-weds, enchanted, singing, loiter in the shadows of an old abbey. Exchanging cries of varied joy, they stop to scatter jasmin petals on the stone where the abbess joins her hands in prayer. Merrily they go their way, pausing for a tender kiss.

En sourdine (In silence)   Fauré
Beneath the soaring branches, let us blend our hearts and souls in the dreaming of the pine and arbutus trees. Then, when night is falling, we shall hear the voice of our despair - the nightingale.

Fleur jetée (Cut flowers)   Fauré
Cut flower, gathered with a song and thrown away in a dream, carry my passion away with the wind. Like you, the hand that has chosen you, now shuns me forever. Oh, poor flower, a while ago so fresh, and tomorrow colorless, let the wind that withers you, wither my heart.

Ici-bas (Down here)   Fauré
Down here all lilacs die - I dream of summer that lasts forever! I dream of kisses that last forever! Down here all men weep for their friendships or their loves ...I dream of couples who remain always together!

La prison (The prison)   Fauré
"La prison" is the lament of one imprisoned. Too late
has he realized that his youth is already wasted, and he
reflects on the simple life as characterized by his lim-
ited view of the outside world.

Le secret (The secret)   Fauré
I wish the morning to ignore the name that I have spoken
to the night. I wish the day to proclaim the love that I
have hidden from the morn. I wish the sunset to forget
the secret that I have shared with the day and carry it
off, with my love, within the folds of its pale robe.

Les berceaux (The cradles)   Fauré
Along the dock ships lie waiting, calmly riding at anchor,
unconscious of the cradles rocked by women's hands.
Yet when the day of parting comes - for women must
weep, and men must try the far horizons - they will feel
their massive hulks drawn back toward shore by the soul
of those distant cradles.

Les roses d'Ispahan (The roses of Ispahan)   Fauré
The roses of Ispahan, the jasmines of Mossul, and the
orange blossoms, have not the fresh fragrance nor the
sweet scent of your breath, pale Leilah! Your lips are
of coral and your light laughter sounds lovelier than the
rippling water. Since all kisses have fled from your
sweet lips, there is no fragrance in the orange tree, no
aroma in the roses. Oh! That your love would come
back to my heart and that again it would perfume the orange blossoms and the roses of Ispahan.

Lydia   Fauré
The golden tresses flow on your rosy cheeks and white
neck. The new day is best; let us forget the tomb. Let
your kisses caress my lips like flowers. A hidden lily
gives forth its perfume no more divinely than you. I
love you and expire when your kisses revive my soul.
Oh, Lydia, give me back my life that I may die again.

Mandoline   Fauré
Gallants who go serenading, and fair ladies who listen to
them, softly murmur to each other underneath the sighing
branches. Here are Tircis and Aminte, or maybe it's

Clitander, and here is Damon, who writes tender verses
for many cruel maidens. Their broidered doublets of
silk, their trailing rustling dresses, their elegance,
their joy, and their soft, faint shadows, whirl together
in the radiance of a rose and silver moonlight, while a
mandoline is tinkling through the breeze.

Nell   Fauré

June, your purple rose sparkles in your brilliant sun.
My heart and your rose are alike. Turtle doves coo
their amorous lament. Sweet is your pearl in the sky,
star of the pensive night! Sweeter is the vivid light
which shines in my charmed heart! The singing sea will
silence its everlasting murmur, 'ere in my heart, lovely Nell, your image will cease to bloom!

Poème D'un Jour (Poem of A Day)   Fauré
1.   Rencontre (Meeting)
I was sad and melancholy when I met you. I feel less
torment today. Tell me, will you be the woman long desired and the dream sought for so vainly? Will you be
the friend who will bring happiness to the lonely poet and
shine on my soul like the native sun on my heart?

2.   Toujours (Always)
You ask me to be silent - to go from you, only, without
remembering whom I love. Ask rather that the stars
fall into the depths, that the night lose her shadows, that
the day lose its brilliance. Ask the sea to absorb the
sobs of the waves. Be sure that my soul never will free
itself from bitter sorrow nor will it lose its fire.

3.   Adieu (Farewell)
As everything dies in a short time, so the rose and all
the other flowers wither; the longing sighs, the beloved
ones vanish! One sees how in this fickle life our dreams
are shifting faster than the waves and our hearts changing
faster than the flakes of frost. I had hoped to be faithful
to you, but even the greatest loves are passing fast.
And almost at the moment of confessing eternal love, I
leave you without tears - farewell!

Le miroir (The mirror)   Ferrari
Your perfume seemed to linger on the silent air. In the
empty room I saw your book on the table and your mirror which shone as the fairest skies of summer. In
blessed memory I bent in quiet prayer and gently kissed
the glass that once mirrored the beauty of your eyes.

L'intruse (The intruder) Février
A Queen would go to a stranger waiting at the palace
gate. "Have care," said the King, "for the new day has
not yet come." The Queen without answering went,
greeted the stranger with a kiss, and silently went away.
The King stands weeping at the palace gate as the dawn
is breaking and as the dead leaves fall.

M'appari tutt 'amor, from "Marta" (You appeared to me full
of love) Flotow
Like a fair dream those hours spent with thee! But
alas, thou art gone and that dream of bliss is o'er.

Carnaval Fourdrain
Carnival, joyous carnival! The trumpets proclaim the
approaching Queen...She rallies her jester, whose lips
are mute...He answers, "Thanks, my love, I can dis-
pense with these lessons. I am listening to the soul of
the city; it rises to greet you through the tumult. See,
the sun mounts, he kisses your hand. O Queen, he illuminates your diadem with his brilliance ."

Chanson norvégienne (Norwegian song) Fourdrain
The dramatic song of a peasant girl, who, betrayed by
her lover, goes to the village dance to try to forget her
grief.

L'oasis (The oasis) Fourdrain
"Deep in the desert is hidden a fragrant spot with green
leaves and mysterious branches; there the breezes sing
night and day and from it runs a spring that quenches all
thirst. Within that cool shade, I may find the dream of
youth long vanished."

Promenade à mule (A mule promenade) Fourdrain
The little mule trots along, dressed in his best harness
and with a bouquet of flowers on each side. The lady
who drives him finds his dreaming makes him move too
slowly, so with a crack of the whip she breaks his reverie and they hurry on to her rendezvous with her lover.

FRANCK
Franck, the Belgian-born French composer, was organist
at Saint Clothilde for nearly forty years. His influence
as a teacher was great, since he had such notable composers as Duparc, d'Indy, Pierné, and Chausson as students. As a composer he received meager appreciation
from his contemporaries, yet he continued to create works
in accordance with his convictions. His music is marked

51

by a mysticism, a simplicity, and an unusual harmonic color.

La procession (The procession)   Franck
God is moving across the fields. He comes, borne by the priests and followed by the people. Birds, join your voices in the hymns of men! They halt. Under an ancient oak the crowd bows before the monstrance. O sun, cast upon him your dying rays. O holy feast! All glows, all prays, and all is fragrance. God is moving across the fields.

Le mariage des roses (Marriage of roses)   Franck
Sweet one, dost thou know how the roses marry? Ah, this union is so charming. What tender things they say on opening their eyes. They say: let us love each other, life is so short. While man on his knees doubts, hopes and prays, my sisters let us embrace." Therefore, beloved, let us love as they do. See, Spring comes to you and to the swallows. To love is the only law - my Queen, follow thy King.

Nocturne   Franck
O cooling, translucent hours of night, you spread a mystic twilight over this dark and monstrous life. O cooling night give of thy peace, I pray.

Panis angelicus (Bread of angels)   Franck
Bread of angels given to men as spiritual food; what a gift for us, the poor and lonely servants, to be nourished by the Lord.

Ninna nanna (Lullaby)   Gargiulo
Lullaby, lullaby. The baby boy sleeps in the cradle with a smile on his lips - like a divine angel, as white as he is dear, truly the god of Love! An Ave Maria ascends to heaven as the mother watches her sleeping love. The bells sound: "Ding! Dong! Dong!"

Duet: Bess, you is my woman, from "Porgy and Bess" Gershwin
From George Gershwin's folk opera, which tells of life in Catfish Row in Charleston, South Carolina, comes this effective duet in which Bess and Porgy pledge their eternal faith and devotion.

La canción al arbol del olvido (The song of the tree of forgetfulness) Ginastera
There is a tree which is known as the tree of forgetful-

ness, and to forget you, I went to sleep under its branches one night. But upon awakening, I thought of you again, as I had forgotten to forget you.

Caro mio ben (My beloved)   Giordani
My beloved, believe me, without thee my heart languishes. Thy faithful one is always sighing - stop being so severe, cruel one.

Amor ti vieta, from "Fedora" (Love prohibits you) Giordano
The betrothed of the beautiful Princess Fedora is brought to her, mortally wounded, and it is hinted that Count Loris has committed the murder. Fedora uses all her skill in fascinating Loris in the hope that she will find proof of his guilt. He has already fallen madly in love with her, and she leads him on, coquettishly, until growing poetic under her enchantment, he tenderly declares that his love is so great and strong that it compels her to love him.

My love prohibits that you should not love. "Tis that light hand that pushes me away which even now is searching for my hand. 'Tis thin own glance that tells me, "I love you!" while thy lips murmur, "I cannot love you!"

Nemico della patria (The enemy of my country), from "Andrea Chenier"   Giordano
With the production of Andrea Chenier at La Scala, in Milan, in 1892, Giordano enjoyed his first success. The scene of this opera is laid in Paris at the time of the French Revolution.

Andrea Chenier, a young poet, is interested in the revolutionary movement. At a ball given by the Countess de Coigny, he meets and falls in love with her daughter, Madeleine. When the revolution breaks out, Chenier tries to save Madeleine and flees with her. He is caught and arrested, and is tried by a Tribunal over which Gerard, a former lackey in the de Coigny home, presides. Madeleine comes to plead with Gerard for Chenier's life. In the aria, "The enemy of my country," Gerard is sorely tempted to relent and to allow Chenier to escape. However, the mob thirsts for Chenier's blood, and he is led off to execution.

Aria of Antonida, from "A Life for the Czar" Glinka
Oh fields, how long must I wait for my dear one? There has been no sign of my love for many a day, but I know he will be coming; my heart tells me so. The joyful

leaves are rustling that my falcon lives and that he will soon be here. I see your little hut in the rosy glow of evening. As your loving wife, I shall enter and all sorrows will vanish. Soon our hands will be joined in marriage.

Aria of Ludmilla, from "Russlan and Ludmilla" Glinka
Ah, kindly star, do not hide your face behind the shades of night. Oh, Ratmir, your mistress waits with love-filled heart; I long for you, my love, my hope. I long for you from hour to hour; when you are near I am joyful. It was in your arms I found protection when I left my father's home. What is life without you? Come back to me!

Aria of Sussanin, from "A Life for the Czar" Glinka
Sussanin, after having lead a group of Polish marauders to a death trap in the snow-covered forest, sings: "They have guessed that death is near to them. Though I too must die, I have no fear, I have done my duty. The coming dawn will be my last. O Lord, give me strength in this hour of need. My beloved family, you will never know where my bones lie. By the winds of the storm I send my petition to Bogdan, to care for my daughter. Vanya, you will be an orphan and your sister will cherish you. Farewell, my children. The Polish soldiers are asleep. I too should forget myself in sleep, which, though calm, will become my final rest."

Barcarolle Glinka
In spite of the calm of night, in the wave is the same anxiety as in my heart. I cannot sleep. When the night descends, my love compels me to take my boat and to row and sing until a magic window opens.

I remember the enchanted moment Glinka
I remember the enchanted moment when you appeared before me. It was a vision, it was the symbol of purest beauty. Long years of life with all kinds of hardships - lonesome - without hope - without faith - made me forget even your image. All of a sudden my soul awoke and I saw you again before me. My heart beat faster - I gained faith - I found my love.

The doubt Glinka
Oh cease, you emotions of passion! Quiet, hopeless heart. I weep and suffer. Because of the unbearable separation my soul is exhausted. I hope this cruel moment will pass away. We will meet again and love and passion will

again embrace us.

Air d'Agamemnon, from "Iphigénie en Aulis"   Gluck
Pitiless Diana, in vain you ordain this horrible sacrifice;
in vain you promise us to be propitious, to let loose for
us the winds shackled by your command. No, outraged
Greece will not be revenged on the Trojans at this price.
I renounce the honors that were destined for me; if it
costs me my life, my daughter, Iphigenia, shall not be
sacrificed...

Che farò senza Euridice?   (What will I do without Euridice?),
from "Orfeo ed Euridice"   Gluck
Orfeo expresses his grief for his wife, Euridice, who
has been doomed by the Gods to die a second time.

Divinités du Styx   (Gods of the lower world)   from
"Alceste"   Gluck
Gods of the lower world, ministers of Death, I shall no
more call upon your cruel pity. I take a tender husband
from his fatal destiny, but I leave you a faithful wife.
To die for the one I love is the sweetest sacrifice.   I
feel a new power: I follow love's call.

O del mio dolce ardor (Oh my sweet ardor), from "Paride
ed Elena"   Gluck
Oh my sweet ardor, my beloved, the air that you breathe,
finally I will breathe. Wherever I look, love shows me
the vague semblance of you. With the desire that fills
my heart, I look for you, I call you, I hope and I sigh.

Recitatif et cavatine de Pylade, from "Iphigénie en Tauride"
Gluck
Pylade, in prison and condemned to death, sings of the
affection he bears for his friend, Orestes, who is awaiting a similar fate. He cautions Orestes to approach
death with becoming dignity. "Death, itself," he says,
"holds no terror since we will be reunited in the tomb."

Ritorna l'età dell'oro (Return golden age), from "Il Trionfo
di Clelia"   Gluck
Return, golden age, back to the abandoned earth that you
have imagined in happy dreams. No, it is not true.
That sweet time did not fly, it is not a dream. Each innocent one feels youth again in his peacefulness.

Spiagge amate (Gentle meadows), from "Paride ed Elena"
Gluck
Gentle meadows, flower-deckt hills where my beloved one

happily walked, silvery brooks which mirrored her beauty, dear springs in which she bathed, tell me, where is she now? Where can I find her?

Vieni, che poi sereno (Come, for thy love is waiting), from "Semiramide" Gluck

Come, thy love is waiting. Come with joy, as the morn is breaking. Banish tears, sadness and envious rivals; find joy and gladness. Happy thou shall ever be.

GOUNOD

Gounod's fame rests largely on the success of his opera, "Faust." After having won the second Prix de Rome, he returned to France and took a two-year course in theology with the idea of entering the priesthood; however, he did not take orders. It is to this facet of his personality that the certain mysticism that pervades his music can be traced. He was primarily a master of voluptuous melody and orchestration.

Avant de quitter ces lieux (Before leaving this place), from "Faust" Gounod

Valentine is pensively examining a medallion which Marguerite, his sister, has given him as a charm to protect him from the dangers of battle. He is to depart with the soldiers that evening and is worried about the welfare of his motherless sister. To a melody of unusual breadth and sweep, Valentine prays for heaven's protection on his sister during his absence.

Ah, je veux vivre (I want to live), from "Roméo et Juliette" Gounod

I want to live in a dream which will intoxicate me for a long time. Sweet flame, I will guard thee in my soul like a treasure. This intoxication of youth only lasts a day, then comes the time when one cries, the heart gives way to love, and joy departs forever. Far away from sad winter, let me sleep and smell the roses before they lose their petals.

Le Roi de Thulé and Air des bijoux (The King of Thulé and Jewel Song), from "Faust" Gounod

As Marguerite is seated at the spinning-wheel, she sings a simple old song that happens to be floating through her mind. It is a quaint old melody, with words telling the time-honored legend of the faithful King of Thulé and his golden goblet. In the midst of her musings, she discovers the casket of jewels left by Mephistopheles on her doorstep. In childlike ecstasy she adorns herself with the gems and all else is forgotten.

Mephistopheles' serenade, from "Faust"   Gounod
   After Marguerite is betrayed and deserted by Faust and
   shunned by her neighbors, Mephistopheles mocks her
   from beneath her window with a villainous and insulting
   serenade. It is a lover's plea to his mistress to open
   her door and has an unmistakable jeering reference to
   the fate of Marguerite... "Lock your heart 'till you have
   a ring."

Salut! demeure chaste et pure (I greet thee, dwelling chaste
and pure), from "Faust"   Gounod
   What unknown feeling penetrates my being? I feel love
   taking possession of me. Oh, Marguerite, here I am at
   your feet. I greet you, dwelling chaste and pure, where
   one feels the presence of an innocent and divine soul.
   What wealth in all this poverty, what happiness is in this
   hidden place. Oh nature, it is here that this girl slept
   under thy guard and grew under thine eyes.

Serenade   Gounod
   When you sing, you recall the most beautiful days of my
   life. When you smile, love blooms and distrust disappears. When you sleep, all earth murmurs harmonious-
   ly, caught in the spell of your charm.

Trio: Prison scene, from "Faust"   Gounod
   The final scene of the opera reveals Marguerite in prison,
   doomed to die for having strangled her child. Faust, accompanied by Mephistopheles, comes to beg her to let him
   save her, but her broken mind cannot return to realities.
   Seeing Mephisto, Marguerite draws back in terror and calls
   to Heaven for protection. As Mephisto drags Faust off into
   the fiery abyss, the soul of Marguerite is borne heavenward.

I'll come, I'll go   Gretchaninoff
   As I go gaily along the highway, I dream of my beloved.
   Will he answer yea or nay? Will he bid me go or stay?

Il s'est tu, le charmant rossignol (You are silent, lovely
nightingale)   Gretchaninoff
   You are silent, lovely nightingale. Stars are gleaming on
   high over the vale and the moonbeams, peering through
   the trees, sparkle on dewdrops of the meadow. Cool and
   restful is the night - is there a whisper? No, there is
   not a sound. It was only a leaf falling at my feet.
   There's the spell of an unknown spring night in your charm,
   my beloved, my own! Ah! Fair night, fairer dream, why

must you ever fade away?

Air from "Les Deux Avares" (The Two Misers)   Grétry
This amusing air is from a comic opera by Grétry, composer of revolutionary France, and friend of Voltaire.

In it the miser berates his relatives, and sends them all
"to the devil" for their avarice. He says, "They are
like a cat who greedily watches the mouse and sharpens
his teeth in anticipation of his feast." Likewise, his
relatives are only waiting for the moment they can fall
upon his money.

Je crains de lui parler la nuit (I fear his words at eve),
from "Richard Coeur de Lion"   Grétry
I fear his words at eve, for when I hear them, my heart
beats wildly. I do not know why. When he presses my
hand tenderly, I am lost as to what to do. I want to
leave him, but I cannot.

Quand l'age vient (When age comes), from "La Fausse
Magie"   Grétry
When age comes, love leaves us, for the young love the
young. Age is a time of wisdom without flattery.

Serenade, from "L'Amant Jaloux"   Grétry
To the accompaniment of a mandoline, a serenader sings
under the window of his beloved Leonore. "Whilst all is
sleeping in the shadows of night, love, who is ever a-
wake, directs my steps. This is the hour of rendezvous."

GRIEG
Grieg rejected the German traditions of his training and
based his style on the folk music of his native Norway.
In his songs, a fresh abundance of melody closely con-
forms to the mood of the lyrics written by poets of the
North. His 135 songs are vital and have a deep poetic
expression. The accompaniments are pictorial, rich in
color, and have unusual modulations.

Der gynger en Baad paa Bolge (A boat rocks on the waves)
Grieg
The lover describes her dear one, who is sailing down
the river to join her, before the boat rounds the bend.

Det fórste Móde (The first meeting)   Grieg
The lover's first meeting is like the moment when the
rays of the sun fall upon roses and bring forth their fragrance. It is like the sound of a horn from a distant

forest which, though it can barely be heard, fills the
heart with yearning.

Ein Traum (A dream)   Grieg
I dreamed of a golden-haired girl in a forest glade.
Here the truth became a dream and the dream became
reality.

En Svane (A swan)   Grieg
My swan, white feathered swimmer, you gave no sign of
song or voice. The elves sang in the deep while you
floated above - listening. When we parted, you died singing - a true swan.

Eros   Grieg
Hear me, ye cold hearts, cherish her who is thine and
whom only ye love. Cherish her with boundless longing
and the fire of passion. Love is the only limitless joy
that men may know.

Fra Monte Pincio, (From Monte Pincio)   Grieg
How mild the night, how red the sky! Everything, enve-
loped in a colorful light, becomes divine; the mountain is
transfigured like a face in death. The peaks shine in the
scented blue distance; dark mists drift over the fields,
hovering like memories, weaving a garment centuries
old. Everything is glowing - the setting sun, crowds of
people, music of horns, scent of flowers, passionate
eyes. In this light and music, everything longs for the
radiance of reconciliation. Now the night grows quieter,
the sky darkens and heaven sees the future taking shape
from the past, forming like a hazy glow in the gathering
darkness. Like a single flame, Rome will rise again
and heal the night of Italy's sorrow. Bells will ring and
cannons roar and the past will return with all its fierce
glory. Sound the wedding song with music of zithers and
flutes, tell the faithful that past and future will be one -
Italy's longing will be answered, and gentler feelings will
waken again.

Hytten (The hut)   Grieg
Not a single bush or tree is in sight. A hut stands alone
on the shore, visited only by the tides. All that can be
seen from it is sky, rocks, and sea; but it is the palace
of happiness because love lives there. It contains neither
silver nor gold, only two lovers who see happiness in
each other's eyes. However poor and small the hut, however bleak the shore, this hut is the palace of happiness
because love is there.

Langs en Aa (At the Brook) Grieg
You trees along the brook, whose branches kiss the
stream, even though its waters wash under your roots
and cause you to fall, like you, I've known warm
kisses that bring grief and dark despair. Fair trees!

Lys Nat (Lucent night) Grieg
Has the sun sunk into the sea in the twilight? Have the
stars seen their reflection there? Is it the glow of a new
day which brightens the fringes of the clouds? Are nights
and dreams ended forever? It is scarcely dark before
light comes again, oh, summer night, how brief you are.

Med en Primula veris (With a primrose) Grieg
May this first spring flower please you, sweetheart; do
not refuse it for the roses which will bloom in summer.
Summer's pleasures are precious, and autumn delights
the heart, but spring is the lovliest season, full of love
and gaiety. Beloved, the early sun of spring shines for
us, so take this flower and give me in exchange your
heart with all its delight.

Med en Vandlilie (With a water-lily) Grieg
See, Maria, I bring you a white blossom from the river.
If you will wear it on your breast, it will dream of being
gently rocked by the streams. Child, your breast is like
the stream for it is dangerous to dream there.

Millom Rosor (Among roses) Grieg
The mother sat with her child among the roses, laughing
and playing, with songs and caresses. She kissed him
and said, "If it please God, I shall see you all my life
among the roses." The birds went away, no songs were
heard among the roses. The boy lay pale and cold in his
coffin. Weeping, the mother laid her wreath upon him,
"Now I shall see you all my life among the roses."

Og jeg vil ha mig en Hjertenskjaer (And I will have me a sweetheart) Grieg
A white horse I will have, and a feather in my hat, and
silken raiment. I shall come riding home, my true-love
with me on St. John's Eve.

Prinsessen (The Prinsessen) Grieg
A fair princess waited in the tower while a shepherd
played his horn in the meadow. "Silence your music, I
pray. It holds my thoughts that would fly away." The
youth, hearing her words, played no more. "Kind shepherd, why are you silent? Your music would carry my

60

thoughts away." Thereupon the youth played again. She wept and sighed, "How wounded my heart, what will happen to me?" Then the sun went down, then the sun went down.

Ragnhild   Grieg
When you came, everything round me spoke a new language; fiord and mountain sang together. And as the boat sailed, it joined in their song. When the journey ended, I could still hear their music. But you said goodbye and went away; the sun sank, the waves stopped singing, the mountains became dumb. But your features did not fade, for I see them in any woman's face where cliffs tower and glaciers spread. Nature itself is but a reflection of Ragnhild.

Solveigs Sang (Solveig's song)   Grieg
One day you will come back and you will be mine. I promised and faithfully wait for you. God help you, wherever you may be, God bless you, when you kneel at His feet. I wait for you, 'till you are at my side. Should you wait for me in heaven, I shall meet you there!

Ved Rundarne (Near Rundarne)   Grieg
Once more I see the hills and valleys of my childhood, spread out before me and bathed in sunshine. I return to the friendly landscape I knew so well, and my youth once more seems near; I return as a child comes to it's mother's breast. And, as though inspired by reaching my goal, I recover the feeling I knew as a child: That there I must stay, that here is my harbor, that fate could grant no kinder gift than that I should live and die in this place.

Monologue from "The Emperor Jones" (Act II)   Gruenberg
The opera, based on a play by Eugene O'Neill, tells the story of the negro convict, Jones, who stowed away to Africa and becomes "Emperor" of a native tribe. This position of eminence gives him the opportunity to commit various crimes and at last to attempt flight to the coast, with much treasure, as the tribe plans to revolt.

Act II deals with Jones' flight through the forest, pursued by his own fears and by the ever-louder, closer and persistent drums of his savage subjects. His gorgeous uniform is in tatters, hallucinations bedevil him and at length, the last shred of bravado leaves him, and he breaks down in a desperate plea to the Almighty for mercy.

Den-bau   Guarnieri
Song without words, just sounds.

La rose y el sauce (The rose and the willow) Guastavino
A rose bloomed in the embrace of a willow. A frivolous
maiden stole the rose - the willow weeps.

D'une prison (From a prison)   Hahn
Above the roof, the sky is blue and quiet; from a tree,
birds are singing - how simple and peaceful is life there!
And you, weeping ceaselessly, what have you done?

L'heure exquise (The exquisite hour)   Hahn
The moonlight glistens on the woods, and from under
every branch, a voice is heard, "Oh, well beloved!"
The lake mirrors the silhouette of a dark willow where
the wind weeps. Let us dream, it is the hour. A vast
and tender calm descends from the heaven to the earth.
It is the exquisite hour.

Paysage (Landscape)   Hahn
I know a hidden place in Brittany, quite near the sea,
where I would love to be with you in autumn. Oaks a-
round a fountain, an old forgotten mill, a spring like the
green reflection of your eyes. The lark would sing for
us in the yellowing branches, and day and night the sea
would accompany our love with its eternal voice.

Si mes vers avaient des ailes (If my poems had wings) Hahn
If my poems had wings, they would fly toward your beautiful garden like a bird! They would float into your
chamber and would remain with you day and night. If
my poems had wings!

Si la rigueur (If hardship), from "La Juive" Halevy
If hardship and revenge turn their success against Thy
holy law, grant forgiveness and mercy, o Lord, and en-
lighten those who turn against you this very day. May
we remember always Thy holy precepts and open our
arms to the child that is lost.

HANDEL
Handel cannot be called a composer of art songs, but had
nearly a thousand solos in his cantatas, operas and oratorios. Described as being unrivaled in his knowledge of
the singer's art, his songs lie well for the voice. His
works always have a strong melodic line and a unique
sublimity and grandeur. He used the "da capo" form in

the majority of his arias. His dramatic sense was an outgrowth of his success in opera. His strong religious feeling is evident in the large number of religious works, of which, "The Messiah" is the most universally popular. Handel was, to his generation, the outstanding composer of Italian opera in Europe - as famous and admired in Italy itself as in his native Germany or in England, the land of his adoption.

Ah, spietato (Oh, cruel one), from "Amadigi" Handel
Oh, cruel one, how you make me suffer! Are you not moved by the love that fills my heart for you alone?

Alma mia (My soul), from "Floridante" Handel
Night, bring back my love. Sometimes I believe my beloved is standing at the door, but - it is only a dream. How long do I have to wait in vain?

Cangiò d'aspetto (How changed life's aspect), from "Admeto" Handel
How changed life's aspect! No longer do I suffer pain and torment - all is turned to joy.

Care selve (Beloved forests), from "Atalanta" Handel
Beloved forests, cool shades, to you I go in search of my beloved.

Dank sei dir, Herr (Thanks be to Thee) Handel
This is a prayer of thanks to the Lord for having led the children of Israel out of bondage in Egypt and through the Red Sea.

Di ad Irene (Go! Call Irene), from "Atalanta" Handel
Go! Call Irene, my cruel, unfaithful mistress. No, it is better to tell her that such love as mine is divine. Where can she ever find another heart like mine? Tell her that my faith is restored when I see the light of love in her beloved eyes.

Dignare (Vouch-safe, o Lord), from "Te Deum" Handel
Vouchsafe, o Lord, this day to keep us without sin. Let Thy mercy be upon us, as we have hoped in Thee.

Lascia ch'io pianga (Leave me to languish), from "Rinaldo" Handel
Leave me to languish, vainly lamenting my lost freedom. I implore Heaven to assuage my pain and anguish.

Let the bright Seraphim, from "Samson"   Handel
This is the famous "Trumpet Aria" from one of Handel's greatest oratorios, "Samson."

Lord, to Thee each night and day, from "Theodora" Handel
The monumental, grandiose, powerful Handel oratorio, with its majestic choral pieces, its lyric arias and its expressive recitative, is the absolute climax of the oratorio idea.   Because of Handel, oratorio came into great prominence in England.

"Theodora" is among the last of his famous English oratorios; it was composed in 1749 and presented the following year.

Non è si vago e bello (Not lovelier nor fairer), from "Julius Caesar"   Handel
The scene is set in Caesar's camp.   Cleopatra enters and bows before him. He asks her: "Who art thou?" She replies: "One of Cleopatra's women." Touched by her gracefulness and beauty he sings: "The flower of the meadow is not as lovely nor as fair as your rare beauty. In the springtime sunshine, your hair radiantly flows beneath your rosy cheeks."

O ruddier than the cherry, from "Acis and Galatea" Handel
In Handel's pastorale, "Acis and Galatea," the shepherd Acis and the nymph Galatea are in love with each other. The giant, Polythemus, also in love with Galatea and jealous of Acis, is determined to disturb the lovers and to kill Acis. He enters with the recitative "I Rage, I Melt, I Burn," and sings the aria "O ruddier than the cherry," which is his idea of a love song.

Oh Sleep, why dost thou leave me, from "Semele" Handel
The plot concerns the old Greek legend of Jupiter's love for Semele, daughter of King Cadmus, Juno's ensuing jealousy, and the vengeance she wreaks upon the hapless Semele.   This aria is sung by Semele when she realizes that, as Juno has been abandoned for her, she too may one day be forsaken.

Ombra mai fu (No shade so rare), from "Serse" Handel
No shade so rare was ever cast upon the brow of a mountain beneath arching boughs.

Perfido! (Unfaithful one!), from "Radamisto"   Handel
Unfaithful one, tell the tyrant that a great soul does not know fear! Tell him that father and son know how to

live and die courageously.

Rendi'l sereno al ciglio (Let peace shine in your eyes), from
"Sosarme"   Handel
Mother, let peace shine in your eyes.   Ah! weep no more.
Fear not; let joy and gladness refreshen your heart.

Sei mia gioia (Thou art my treasure), from "Parthenope"
Handel
Thou, my blessing and my treasure, all my hope and
peace I owe to thee.

Si, tra i ceppi (Even chained), from "Berenice"   Handel
Even chained and tortured, my faith is invincible.   Nor
will death extinguish my belief.

Sommi Dei (Supreme Gods), from "Radamisto"   Handel
Written in London in 1720, "Radamisto" was the eleventh
of Handel's 46 operas.   Either outmoded or obscured by
other numbers, it is today all but forgotten, although biographers speak of it as a masterpiece.   Polissena's
aria is a superb piece of lyric declamation, with which
the opera opens; it is an invocation to the Gods for protection.   "Great Gods, good Gods! Gods of all mercies.
Look upon my pain.   See my tears and have pity."

HAYDN
Haydn, known as the "father of the symphony," and
credited with an immense amount of instrumental music,
was equally successful in writing for the voice, as attested by his oratorios and a number of charming songs.
As an accompanist, in early years, to the great singing
teacher, Porpora, he gained a knowledge of the voice
which is apparent in all of his songs and arias.   There
is a gentle happiness in Haydn's music and a subtle feeling of folk music.

Cara spéme (Dear Hope), from "Orpheus ed Euridice" Haydn
Oh, return to me, heart of my heart, my beloved Euridice.   Sweet hope, come to my aid.   No one knows my
anguish - even the forest echoes to my despair.

Mermaid's Song   Haydn
Now, when the sunbeams play on the glassy sea, I will
lead you to where the pearly treasures lie beneath the
rolling waves.   Come with me before the storms blow
and the tide changes to the ocean caves where the coral
grows.

My mother bids me bind my hair   Haydn
This song is the lament of a maid whose mother insists
that she should "bind her hair," wear gay raiment, and
join the young people in their fun. But alas, she has no
spirit for this as her lover is now far away.

She never told her love   Haydn
Words from Shakespeare's "Twelfth Night."

The spirit's song   Haydn
Listen, my beloved, do not sorrow over my tomb. My
spirit waits until you come. I see you weeping upon the
stone over my cold ashes. I watch each falling tear and
hear your sighs before they fade away in the air.

With verdure clad, from "The Creation"   Haydn
This is a familiar excerpt from Haydn's great oratorio,
with the following text:

And God said, "Let the earth bring forth grass, the herb
yielding seed, and the fruit tree yielding fruit after his
kind, whose seed is in itself, upon the earth." And it was
so. With verdure clad, the fields appear, delightful to
the ravish'd sense; by flowers sweet and gay, enhanced
is the charming sight, here fragrant herbs their odors
shed, here shoots the healing plant. With copious fruit
the expanded boughs are hung, in leafy arches twine, the
shady groves, o'er lofty hills majestic forests wave.

Au pays (Returning home) Holmès
A soldier marches home at the head of his battered bat-
talion, hungry, yet merry. "Ah! there's my home,
that's my village. There my pretty girl is waiting...
My Jeannette, tell me you are still faithful to me." "Bah!
I married a long time ago. Go away now! It's not my
fault, poor fellow; they told me you would never return."
"So, it is over? Then back to battle! To battle!"

Mimaamaquim (Psalme CXXX)   Honegger
Oh Lord, out of the depths of my heart I cry to thee!

Trois Psaumes (Three Psalms)   Honegger
1. Psalm 34
I will bless the Lord at all times, His praise shall con-
tinually be in my mouth. My soul shall make her boast
in the Lord; the meek shall hear thereof, and be glad.

2. Psalm 40
Deliver me, O Lord, from the evil man. Preserve me

from the violent man.

3. Psalm 138
I will give Thee thanks with my whole heart, I will sing
praises to Thee. I will give thanks unto Thy holy name
for Thy loving kindness and truth.

À des oiseaux (Message to the birds)   Hüe
Good morning, pretty thrushes, pretty chaffinches. A-
waken the brook and the flowers. Take care, little birds,
soar high, do not touch the earth, for some little children are waiting to catch you. Take what you will of my
fruits and flowers. Good night, pretty thrushes, pretty
chaffinches. Sing the brook and flowers to sleep.

J'ai pleuré en rêve (Dreaming, I wept)   Hüe
I wept, beloved, when I dreamed that you had left this
vale. Tears burst from my eyes as I dreamed you had
forsaken me. And when I woke I sobbed, knowing that
your heart was still aglow. Blind were my eyes with
tears that ever flowed.

Madrigal   Indy
Indy's place in French music is bes understood if he is
pictured as the successor of his teacher, César Franck.
But he differs from Franck in that he is more analytical,
more intellectual, and, on the other hand, he responds to
a wide variety of external stimulae, such as the delights
of Nature and the charm of regional folksongs.

Le thé (The tea)   Koechlin
Miss Ellen, pour the tea into the cup where the gold-fish
quarrel with a pink monster. I love the cruelty of tam-
ing the lion-headed serpent. Miss Ellen, pour the tea into the lovely Chinese cup.

Si tu le veux (If you like)   Koechlin
If you like, my beloved, let us wander into the dark and
lovely night, only the two of us, unseen by others. Then
I will sing to you many lovesongs and they will tell you
of my heart's happiness. When you return home, if
someone should ask you, "why is it that your hair is loose
and in disorder?" Answer that the wind has disarranged
it. If you like, my beloved.

Marietta's Lied (Marietta's song), from "Die Tote Stadt"
Korngold
My only joy, my beloved, come close to me. Evening
descends - thou art my light and day. Hearts beat to-

gether, hope wings heavenward. How true, this song of
the true lover who must die. I know also the other
verse of the song: when sorrow approaches, come close
to me, beloved. Bend your pale face to me, death will
not separate us. When you must go from me, believe -
there is a resurrection.

O Mistress Mine   Korngold
("Twelfth Night," Act II, Sc. III)
    Sir Toby and Sir Andrew demand a love-song from the
    Clown, while they enjoy their midnight stoup of wine.

Aubade (Morning serenade), from "Le Roi d'Ys"   Lalo
    They try to discourage me in vain, for I wish to remain
    near to your door. Though the sun may darken and the
    light of day be replaced by night, I will always remain,
    uncomplaining, unaccusing. I know your soul is gentle
    and that the hour will come when your repulsing hand
    will welcome me. Do not be long in relenting, Rosenn,
    else I die!

Che fiero costume (What a fierce manner)   Legrenzi
    What a strange thing for blind Cupid to compel our love
    to withstand such torment! Why should the Fates decree
    such a high place of favor for one that is blind. He is
    a tyrant that insists on persistent suffering. He has
    captured my vision and forces me to sigh!

Chanson à manger (Song to eating)   Lemaire
    An epicure, tired of the eternal songs in praise of drink-
    ing, intones a canticle of the delights of eating - "I lose
    my reason when I drink, find it again when I eat."

Prologue, from "I Pagliacci"   Leoncavallo
    Before the rise of the curtain, Tonio, one of the come-
    dians in I Pagliacci, appears and sings the famous Pro-
    logue, asking the audience's favor and pointing out the
    similarities between real life and the little comedy that
    is to be acted on the stage.

Vesti la giubba (Put on your costume), from "I Pagliacci"
Leoncavallo
    I am delirious, not knowing what I'm saying or doing.
    Yet I must force myself to play the part. Are you not a
    man? You are a clown. Put on your coat and cover
    your face with flour; the people are paying and want to
    laugh. If Harlequin steals Columbine, you must laugh,
    Pagliaccio, and everyone will applaud. Turn into jokes
    the spasms and the tears, and into grimaces the sobbing

of pain. Laugh, Pagliaccio, at your broken love, laugh at the suffering which is poisoning your heart.

La fontaine de Caraouet (The fountain of Caraouet)   Letorey
The fountain of Caraouet murmurs in a verdant bower. He who drinks from it can make a wish and forget.

Canta il mare (Song of the sea)   De Leva
In the starlit night the song of the sea mingles with my dreams. From afar the wave sings, "Dearest, April now returns! It is the time for love!"

Comment disaient-ils?   (What did they say?)   Liszt
The accompaniment portrays the dialogue of the characters in the poem. "How can we escape the alguazils?" She answers, "Row, swiftly row." "How can we forget our perils?" She replies, "Sleep, only sleep." He asks, "How can I win a gentle maiden?" She replies, "By love, tender love."

Es muss ein Wunderbares sein (It must be wonderful)   Liszt
It must be a wonderful thing, indeed, when two hearts confide and trust in each other, with no thought of hiding.

Oh, quand je dors (Oh, when I sleep)   Liszt
Oh, when I sleep, come to me as Laura came to Petrarch; and when my heart is heavy with grief, by thy presence banish all its sadness, and teach me the happiness of love.

Pur dicesti (Say to me)   Lotti
Say to me, oh beautiful lips, the sweet word, "yes," which delights me. Amor, holding his torch high, with a kiss will make thee succumb.

Arioso, from "L'Armide"   Lully
Begone from me, all pleasure. Armide, alone, can bring you back. Without the spell of her beauty, everything is pain.

Bois épais (Sombre woods), from "Amadis"   Lully
Lully, the first of the great French composers, enjoyed the favor of the Court all his life. He was appointed court composer in 1653 and wrote masques and ballets in which Louis XIV himself took part. Lully also, as "M. Baptiste," danced and acted in the court ballets and festival-plays, and made himself indispensable to the King, who preferred his music to all other.

His real fame - that of creating French opera - dates from 1672, when he obtained letters patent for the establishment of an "Académie royale de musique." His operas held the stage for nearly a century until Gluck's grander creations overwhelmed them.

"Sombre woods, in your shadows hide my unhappy love. If I will never again see my beloved, then I will forever hate the light."

Il faut passer tôt ou tard (Soon or late, all must go), from "Alceste" Lully
In the dismal regions where courses the river Acheron, Charon, the ferryman of the dead, plies his gloomy trade:

"Be it soon or late - all must board my boat. Youth and age, king and shepherd, I receive all of you on equal terms..."

Revenez, revenez, amours (Return, love), from "Thésée" Lully
Why leave this peaceful place where pleasure has followed our steps? Do you love me no more? O, return to me, for without love nothing gives pleasure.

Ave Maria   Luzzi
O holy Virgin, full of grace, blessed among women, hear my prayer.

MAHLER
Mahler was one of four children in a large family that lived to adulthood. It was his misfortune to see and to know much tragedy. This experience is reflected in most of his 42 songs which, many authorities feel, contain his best writing. Much of his music is soul searching, filled with excitement and tension. One of the greatest conductors he had a superb knowledge of the virtuoso voice as a musical instrument.

Blicke mir nicht in die Lieder (Do not look at my songs) Mahler
Do not look at my songs! I myself lower my eyes, feeling as though it were evil to watch them grow. Do not look at my songs! Your curiosity seems like treason. Bees, building their cells, will not allow anyone to watch them. They do not look themselves, when the sweet honeycombs are brought to light. You will be the first to taste their sweetness.

Der Tamboursg'sell (The drummer boy)   Mahler
A poor drummer boy am I. They take me out of the cell.
Had I stayed a drummer, I would not have been in prison. Oh high gallows, how fearsome you are. I cannot
look at you, for there I shall hang. The soldiers marching by, will ask who I have been: drummer boy of the
regiment's first company. Farewell you officers, cor-
porals and musketeers. I take my leave of you! Farewell!

Ich atmet' einen linden Duft (I breathed a gentle fragrance)
Mahler
I breathed a gentle fragrance. In the room stood a branch
of linden, a gift from your dear hand. How wonderful is
the odor of the sprig you gently gathered! I softly
breathe the fragrance of love's gentle scent.

Ich bin der Welt abhanden gekommen (I am lost to the world)
Mahler
I am lost to the world, where I once lost so much time.
It has not heard from me for ages, and may believe I
am dead. I do not care, if it thinks I have died. I will
not contradict, for in reality I have died, died to this
world. I have gone from the world's turmoil and rest in
quiet solitude. I live in my heaven, in my love, in my
song.

Kindertotenlieder (Songs On The Death Of Infants) Mahler
1. Nun will die Sonn' so hell aufgeh'n! (Once more the sun
would gild the morn!)
Once again, the sun gilds the morn as though the night
had hidden no harm. But I must weep and mourn, even
though the sun shines. Do not surrender to grief, the dark
of night foretells the day and the splendor of light. A little
lamp has died in my heart. Let us praise the joyous light of
the world.

2. Nun seh' ich wohl, warum so dunkle Flammen (Now I know
why dark flames came from your eyes)
Now I know why sometimes dark flames came from your
eyes - to express in one glance their whole power. But as
fate blinded me, I did not know that they went home - from
where all rays come. You wanted to tell me: we like to
stay near you! But fate did not permit. Look at us - soon
we are away! What today are only eyes to you - in future
nights they will be stars.

3. Wenn dein Mütterlein (When thy mother dear)

When your mother enters, and I turn to greet her, I do
not look into her sad face. First I lower my eyes to
the door, where I search in vain for your infant face.
How the father used to rejoice to hear your voice. Each
time your mother enters, I think I hear the patter of
your feet. Alas, a father's and mother's treasure has
departed.

4. Oft denk' ich, sie sind nur ausgegangen! (I think oft',
they've only gone for a walk!)
    I often think they have gone for a walk and that I'll see
    them coming home again. The day is bright. Only one
    step before us, they have gone to yonder height. Soon
    we will follow. How bright the day there!

5. In diesem Wetter! (In such bad weather!)
    Never would I have permitted the children to go out in such
    bad weather. They have been carried away - I could not
    say a word. In such bad weather they rest and sleep as
    in mother's arms. No storm can frighten them now.
    They are with God and under His protection.

Liebst du um Schönheit (If you love for beauty...) Mahler
    If you love for beauty, love the golden sun. If you love
    for youth, cherish the spring. If you love for treasure,
    woo the mermaid who has many glistening pearls. If
    you love for love, then love me always, for I shall love
    you forever.

Lieder eines fahrenden Gesellen (Songs of a wayfarer) Mahler
1. My sweetheart makes wedding preparations to marry an-
    other. I go to my dreary room and weep for love. The
    birds sing, "What a beautiful world, cheer up." Sing no
    more, birds. Bloom no more, flowers. Spring has al-
    ready flown.

2. This morning as I crossed a dew covered meadow, a merry
    finch sang to me, 'Hello there! Good morning! What a
    beautiful world." The bluebells toned with their bells,
    "Kling, kling. What a beautiful world." The whole world
    began to glisten. Can my happiness ever return? No,
    this can never be.

3. I have a burning knife in my breast that cuts so deep. It
    cuts deep into joy and happiness. It gives neither rest nor
    sleep - in daytime or at night. If I look into the heavens, I
    see two blue eyes. When I go through the fields, I see her
    blond hair caressed by the wind. When I awake from my

dreams, I hear her silvery laughter. - How I long to
lie on the black bier in eternal sleep.

4. The two blue eyes of my sweetheart have sent me into a
   lonely world. Why did you gaze upon me now I have
   eternal sorrow and grief. As I departed at night, no one
   bade me farewell. By the road stood a linden tree, there I
   slept peacefully for the first time covered by its blossoms,
   and forgot life's suffering. All was well again - love and
   sorrow and world and dream.

Rheinlegendchen (Rhine legend)   Mahler
    I mow by the Neckar, I mow by the Rhine. Sometimes
    I have a sweetheart, sometimes I am alone. How can I
    mow if the sickle doesn't cut; what good is a sweet-
    heart if she doesn't stay with me? I throw my golden
    ring into the water and it will move to the ocean. A
    fish will gulp it, which soon will be eaten by the King.
    When the King asks, "Whose ring is this?," my sweet-
    heart will answer, "it's mine!" And then she will bring
    the ring back to me. "Mow by the Neckar, mow by the
    Rhine, but throw into them your ring for me to catch!"

Um Mitternacht (At midnight)   Mahler
    At midnight I am on guard and look at the sky. No star
    shines to bring consolation. At midnight, I trust the power
    in your hands, Lord over life and death, You are standing
    on guard.

Wer hat dies Liedlein erdacht (Who created this little song?)
Mahler
    I see a sweet lass in the window of a house on a hill.
    She is the innkeeper's daughter, and for her my heart is
    full sore. Her brown eyes and rosy lips will cure hearts
    and restore life to the dying. Who created this little
    song? Three geese have brought it over the water - two
    gray ones and a white one. And if a person cannot sing
    the song, they will whistle it for him!

Wo die schönen Trompeten blasen (Where the beautiful trum-
    sound)   Mahler
    "Who softly knocks on the door to awake me? "It is your
    beloved, let me come in so that I can be with my sweet-
    heart as the sun arises." The maiden opened the door
    and gave him her snow-white hand. In the distant valley
    the nightingale sang. The maiden began to weep. "Weep
    not, dear one, for next year you will be my own. I go

to war where the beautiful trumpets are sounding. There is my house of green turf."

Quella fiamma, che m'accende (This flame, lighted in me) Marcello
My beautiful ardour, I will never change, for your dear eyes will always burn. The flame which has been lighted in my heart will never be extinguished.

Sechs Monologe aus "Jedermann" (Six monologues from "Everyman") Frank Martin
1. Ist als zu End das Freudenmahl (The banquet is ended)
The banquet is ended and Everyman is required to stand before his God in judgement. Friends desert him, and finding no help, he turns to lonely meditation.

2. Ach Gott, wie graust mir vor dem Tod (Oh Lord, how I fear death)
His calls to friends have been in vain. He expresses anxiety but with no avail except to ask, "Where am I, rich Everyman." He throws himself on his treasure chest, but Mamon comes from the chest and tells him to go on without clothing, as he was born.

3. Ist als wenn eins gerufen hätt (It is as someone called)
Good Deeds tells him that Everyman's old mother is too weak to go with him.

4. So wollt ich ganz zernichtet sein (So will I be destroyed)
Everyman repents and falls to the earth.

5. Ja! ich glaub: solches hat er vollbracht (Yes, I believe, this He accomplished)
Faith questions Everyman and asks, "Doest thou know Jesus Christ died and rose again that thou might live?"

6. O ewiger Gott! (O eternal God!)
He prays to God and is redeemed and goes to the grave confident of redemption.

Plaisir d'amour (Joy of love) Martini
The joy of love lasts but a moment, the suffering of love lasts all through life. I left everything for the ungrateful Sylvia, but she left me and took another lover. She often said: "Like the water running smoothly towards the river at the edge of the desert, I will always love thee." The water still flows, but she has changed.

Voi lo sapete (You know it), from "Cavalleria Rusticana"
Mascagni
Dear mother, you know that before Turiddu went to war,
Lola and he were ardently in love. When he returned to
find her married to another, I became his chosen one.
Soon, I saw his heart was again burning for Lola and
our bliss was turned to misery. Our love is dead and
so is my honor.

Der Ton (The tone)   Marx
When night leans silently on the window casement, I am
like a monarch, for a rich golden tone sings within me,
telling of the wonders of the firmament. My heart o'er-
flows with happiness.

Hat dich die Liebe berührt (If love has touched you)   Marx
If love has touched you, God will safely guide you. Lost
in dreams you go, leaving others to their pleasures.
You cannot deny that the crown of life adorns your brow.

Selige Nacht (Blissful night)   Marx
Joseph Marx, a Viennese composer, has written some of
the finest of modern Lieder. This song, "Blissful Night,"
presents him in a mood of emotional exaltation. The poem, by Hartleben, tells that

"We gently fell asleep in the arms of love. Through the
open window the summer wind seemed to carry our soft
breath away in the moonlight. From the garden, perfume of roses was wafted about our couch, and gave us
wonderful dreams of beauty, dreams so rich with longing."

Und gestern hat er mir Rosen gebracht (Yesterday he brought
me roses)   Marx
Yesterday he brought me roses - they perfumed the air
the whole night through. They pleaded for him who
thinks of me and I gave him the dream of a night. Today I walk and silently smile and wear his roses and
wait at the door. My heart beats - oh, come to me. I
kiss the roses he brought to me and wander and search
for the dream of the night!

MASSENET
Massenet, during his lifetime, was widely popular as an
opera composer. His music, frequently composed with
the artists in mind who would be appearing before the public in his creation, has an immediate appeal because of
a flowing, voluptuous vocal line, and orchestral treatment.
His opera "Manon" remains prominent in the present day

75

repertory.

Ah, fuyez douce image (Oh, begone tender dream), from "Manon" Massenet
Oh, begone, tender dream, though my soul may torment the peace I have won. The draught I drained was bitter and full of anguish. If only I could forget the one fatal name that haunts me still. O Lord, cleanse my soul with fire and dispel, with your heavenly light, the gloom that lives in my heart. Oh, begone, tender dream, leave my soul forever.

Chant Provençal (Country song) Massenet
Mirella isn't yet aware of the sweet charm of her beauty! It is a flower that came to blossom in summer's smile. From him, who knows not Mirella, God's dearest treasure is hidden! Her grace, beyond compare, adorns her better than a mantel of gold. Nothing disturbs the chaste dream of her innocent and pure heart. She smiles at the dawning day; the azure day smiles at her. Mirella isn't yet aware of the sweet charm of her beauty! It is a flower that came to blossom in summer's smile.

Élégie (Elegy) Massenet
Spring is gone forever! Never shall I see the blue sky, no more listen to the gay songs of the birds! My happiness is gone with you! Spring returns in vain. Without you, the sun is dark, the happy days are gone forever!

En ferment les yeux (While closing my eyes), from "Manon" Massenet
Sweet moment, when fear has passed, and we two are alone. Listen, Manon, on my way I had a dream. When I close my eyes, I see a humble dwelling, a little white house at the back of the woods. Beneath those tranquil shades, the clear brooks join with the birds in song. That is paradise! But all is sad and morose, for one thing is missing. Manon, come, this would be our life, if you but will, oh Manon.

Hérode, ne me refuse pas (Herod, do not refuse me), from "Hérodiade" Massenet
The wicked Hérodias, one-time favorite of Herod, comes to him, crying out for vengeance against the Prophet, who has insulted her by calling her Jezebel. Herod refuses, and her renewed scoldings are then interrupted by the entrance of John, who denounces them both in such terrifying language that they flee.

Il est doux, il est bon (He is sweet, he is good), from
"Hérodiade"   Massenet
  The Prophet is here, whose word brings relief. He is
  gentle and good. I suffered, I was alone, but his tender
  and melodious voice put my heart at ease.   Beloved
  Prophet, how can I live without thee!

Duet: Il faut nous séparer (We must separate), from
"Werther"   Massenet
  Although not Massenet's most popular work, it is be-
  lieved by many biographers that "Werther" is his best.
  The subject, particularly adapted to the composer's geni-
  us, inspired him to write some of his finest melodies.
  The opera is founded on Goethe's melancholy and ro-
  mantic story of his own life, "The Sorrows of Werther."
  The duet, sung by Charlotte and Werther, dramatically
  tells of their love and despair at parting.

Letter scene, from "Werther"   Massenet
  Charlotte re-reads letters from her old love, Werther.
  She still loves him, though she has sent him away for-
  ever. Werther writes he will return to her on Christ-
  mas day, but adds, "if I do not come, accuse me not!
  Weep for me!"

Ouvre tes yeux bleus (Open your blue eyes)   Massenet
  A song of two lovers. He sings, "Open your blue eyes,
  morn has come. The lark sings and Aurora, with her
  roses, colors the sky. The buds are opening their hearts:
  awake my love." She answers, "The love that is dawning is fairer than the birds and Aurora. In my heart a
  lark is singing and a life-bringing sun is within my
  breast."

Pleurez, mes yeux (Weep, my eyes), from "Le Cid" Massenet
  The Cid (Roderigo Diaz de Rivar) was a Spanish warrior
  of the XIth Century, and the story of his military prowess
  has become traditional in Spain. "Pleurez mes Yeux" is
  sung by Chimene (Act III) as she sits alone, in despairing reverie, in her chamber at night, mourning for her
  father who has been slain by the hand of her lover:
  Roderigo. "The strife is ended, and I turn, broken in
  spirit, to my lonely grief. Weep, my eyes, and flow,
  sad tears. If a hope yet remains, it is that death is
  near. Then flow ye tears - endlessly flowing!"

Pourquoi me reveiller (Why do you wake me), from "Werther"
Massenet
  Werther comes to bid farewell to Charlotte (Act III) and

77

noticing the poems of Ossian on the table, sings the
Gaelic poet's famous ode and reminds Charlotte of the
happy days when together they translated the beautiful
odes. - "Oh, wake me not, you breath of spring, let me
dream on as one who knows bleak winter, with its chill
and sorrows, and dreads awakening. The stranger found
me fair to see and now, in scorn, he passes me to see
so sad a thing!"

Vision fugitive (Fleeting Vision), from "Hérodiade"   Massenet
This potion could bring me a vision of her, in all her
beauty. O divine and overpowering image, cheer my
heart, ensnare my reason, stay with me. If I could only
clasp the fleeting vision, the mysterious angel that con-
trols my being. For this love I would give eternal life.

Hills of Gruzia   Mednikoff
The poem for this song is by Pushkin, and tells of the
love of the homeland, the yearning for the hazy hills
where the light of day was first seen.

Frühlingslied (Spring song)   Mendelssohn
Spring is here! The skies are blue and the fields are
drying. The birds in the woods are calling for their
mates. And I take a bouquet of violets to my love.

Suleika   Mendelssohn
Oh Westwind! Your cool breath awakens longing for my
beloved. Hurry to him and tell him how I suffer in his
absence. Your gentle breath comforts my lonely heart.
Go to my beloved! Speak to him - but not of my anguish.
Tell him that his love is my life and that I yearn for
his return.

La maison grise (The gray house), from "Fortunio"   Messager
I love the old gray house and the hearth where I spent
my youth. The old familiar things welcome my return
and recall many fond memories.

Ah! mon fils (Ah, my son), from "Le Prophète"   Meyerbeer
Ah, my son, be blessed. Your loving mother was dearer
to you than your sweetheart. You alone have given your
mother more than life, the joy of your soul. May
Heaven's blessing be with you forever.

Nobles Seigneurs (Noble Gentlemen), from "Les Huguenots"
Meyerbeer
Noble gentlemen, I greet you. A noble and wise lady,
of whom kings could be jealous, has given me this mes-

sage for you. I give this letter to the gentleman that
she has chosen, but I will not name her. Noble Sirs,
may God protect your wars and your loves.

Nonnes qui reposez (You nuns, who are sleeping), from
"Robert le Diable" Meyerbeer
Robert has come to Sicily where he has fallen in love
with the beautiful princess, Isabella, and she with him.
Bertram does his best to interfere with the match and
keeps Robert from attending the tournament whose winner
is supposed to claim Isabella's hand. Robert, it seems,
has lost his chance to win her and is led by Bertram to
the ruins of a convent. It is here, in the middle of the
night, that Bertram summons the ghosts of faithless
nuns, singing the impressive invocation: "You nuns, who
are sleeping."

Ombre légère (Shadow song), from "Dinorah" Meyerbeer
Come quickly, shadow, and take your lesson from my
dance and song. Do not go away, dreamy and fairy
creature, for it will grieve me if you depart. I rejoice
to see you each morning. Stay and dance to my voice,
sing with me. Ah, tis well. You know that Hoël loves
me and that today God approves me as his loving bride.
The night comes, do not go away! Return, you cruel
one, do not flee! Tarry here! Ah!

O Paradiso (O paradise), from "L'Africana" Meyerbeer
Meyerbeer's most lyrical opera is based on the historical
character, Vasco da Gama, the Portuguese explorer.

I greet thee, wonderful land, delightful groves, and radiant temple. O paradise, arisen above the waves, you belong to me. Must I die at this moment of triumph, to
leave no trace? Lead me to the vessel with the bright
gleaming sails, that I can tell my friends of my success.
May Europe and my native country know that Vasco the
conqueror has laid down his life on these shores. It is
like dying twice to lose both life and immortality. Let
us die like heroes and Christians. O God, receive and
protect me.

Recitative and Aria from "Dinorah" Meyerbeer
Hoël rescues the demented Dinorah from a torrent and
sings this delightful aria to her while she is still unconscious, praying that she return to her senses so that
they may be happy in their love once more.

79

Robert! toi que j'aime (Robert, you whom I adore), from
"Robert le Diable" Meyerbeer
   The plot of this opera concerns Robert, Duke of Nor-
   mandy, son of the Princess Bertha, and Satan, whom she
   knew in human form. Robert has inherited, from his
   father, the evil spirit who, disguised, appears in his life
   and goes under the name of Bertram. The fiend tries
   constantly to lead Robert into evil ways and thus win his
   soul. The mother's good influence is with him in the
   form of his foster sister, Alice. Banished from Nor-
   mandy, because of wicked deeds inspired by Bertram,
   Robert comes to Sicily where he meets and falls in love
   with the Princess Isabella, and she with him. Bertram,
   however, makes every effort to prevent their marriage.
   He leads Robert, at midnight, to a ruined convent, and
   summoning the ghosts of the faithless, tries to persuade
   Robert to sign over his soul. Alice saves him by recalling his mother's warning that Bertram is none other than
   his own evil father. Alice brings Isabella to the cathedral to marry Robert, and, as he is still hesitating, the
   magic hour of twelve is struck by the clock and Bertram
   disappears while Robert enters the church to marry Isabella.

Pinhão quente (Peddler's song - roasted pinecones) Mignone
   Roasted pine cones for sale, my friends, good and hot,
   mulatta. Roasted pine cones, so hot they burn, hey, how
   hot they are!

Quatre Chants Hébraïques (Four Hebrew songs) Milhaud
1. Berceuse (Lullaby)
   Sleep, your papa will go to the village and bring back an
   apple and caress your little head. He will bring back a
   nut and caress your little foot. He will bring back a
   duck and caress your little hands. He will bring back
   soup and caress your little tummy. Sleep, sleep.

2. Chant du veilleur (Song of the watchman)
   I, the sad watchman, go through the night shunning sleep.
   Holà, who is there? Am I made of iron? All others
   are in sleep, but I search for rest on the stones. Holà
   - who goes there?

3. Chant hassidique (Song of a Jewish mystic)
   What can I say to you, and what can I tell you, who can
   tell you and explain to you the meaning of one-two-three-
   four-five-six-seven? Seven, that's the Sabbath, and Six
   the parts of the Talmud, and Five the parts of the Bible,
   and Four the Ancestors, and Three the Patriarchs, and

Two the Tables of the Law, and One is our God, is our
only God. There is no one equal to Him, our God is
one.

4. Gloire à Dieu (Glory to God)
My Lord is my strength and my tower, and I am so poor.
All my hope is in God, and all my confidence is in Him, my
God, my God Sabaoth. I am burned alive, pierced
through by an arrow of fire, by my Lord, by my God.
He has pierced my heart and in my heart has burned my
arrogance and my pride, Lord Sabaoth.

L'hora grisa (At dusk)   Mompou
Everything is asleep during the gray hour, the trees,
the mountains, the birds and the wind! Only the smoke
slowly unfurls upward with the prayers. Later, when
the sky turns serene, a golden star will shine.

MONTEVERDI
Monteverdi, by his innovations in opera, influenced his
successors for many centuries. He envisioned opera as
a dramatic expression of human passion which embraced
all of the arts. To vitalize expression, he used the in-
tonation of impassioned speech in the vocal line. In the
accompaniment, he had a revised orchestra participate
in the dramatic action, utilizing such new effects as dissonance, orchestral tremolo and pizzicato.

Lasciatemi morire (Let me die)   Monteverdi
Let me die. What can bring me comfort in this hour of
a martyr's torment? Let death now take me.

Oblivion soave (Slumber gently), from "L'Incoronazione di
Poppea"   Monteverdi
From one of Monteverdi's most important works comes
this exquisite lullaby, sung to the Empress Poppea. "May
quiet peace and sweet thoughts be with thee in sleep,
child." Rest, oh thieving eyes! Open - what would you
do, when even closed, you steal my love! Poppea,
sleep on in peace, sleep - sleep!"

Qual honor dite sia degno (What honor can be worthy of you),
from "Orfeo"   Monteverdi
What honor can be worthy of you, all-powerful lyre of
mine, which within the realms of darkness moved all
hearts?

Rosa del ciel (Rose of heaven), from "Orfeo"   Monteverdi
Sun, oh burning heart of heaven, source of life to all

the world, proudest work of the Creator, sun who turns above all lands, you whose glance encompasses from star-strewn paths all life, all times - tell me, lives, or lived there ever a man more blessed by love than I?

Tu se' morta (You are dead), from "Orfeo"   Monteverdi
How can you leave this life, beloved, and leave me breathing? How can you steal away, never to return, and leave me in my loneliness?

Vi ricorda, o boschi ombrosi (Wooded shades, do you recall), from "Orfeo"   Monteverdi
O wooded shades, do you recall my long and cruel love torments? The very stones, their hardness melted, made moving answer to my plaints.

MOUSSORGSKY

Moussorgsky, according to Kurt Schindler, was one of the greatest innovators and prophets of modern music. Practically self-taught, he sought for a realistic manner of composition by which he could convincingly communicate the emotions of the human heart. His 66 songs are studies of psychology and are correct in declamation even to the slightest inflection of the spoken word. His melodic line is bold, rugged and frank, while his rhythm and harmony are very free. He chose to write songs about many unconventional subjects.

Aria of Martha, from "Khovantchina"   Moussorgsky
I, an innocent maiden, went through new-mown, wind-dried rushes, through fields and marshes. My feet are cold and torn by brambles. I hastened to find love but I have not found it. Then I'll creep to the house of my dear one and tap on the window. I'll ask, "Don't you remember me? Have you forgotten me? My heart has yearned for you and I long to hear your voice. Like the lights near an altar, our hearts have met in one flame. You were false and disloyal to me; you left me alone to die. The time is near when my vengeance shall follow your cruelty."

At the river Don   Moussorgsky
At the Don is a garden full of roses. There, one evening, I saw lovely Masha. Never shall I forget her tender smile. Distracted, she overturned her pitcher.

Hopak   Moussorgsky
I'm the wife of a Cossack. Ah, sad fate! I'll drown my grief in drinks - one, two, three. He can wash and feed the child. Bah!

Little Star   Moussorgsky
Where did you go, little star, did a dark cloud hide
you? Where are you, my sweet love, did you leave me?
Yes, the dark cloud hid the star and the earth has
covered my love.

Monologue of Boris, from "Boris Godounoff"   Moussorgsky
Boris is an historical personage who ascended the throne
of Russia suspected of having murdered the rightful heir.
In the famous Monologue, he reflects upon his supremacy
in power, on the prophecies of the astrologers for a long
and glorious reign; he finds no solace for his aching
heart in the signs of material greatness and trembles at
the ugly rumors which brand him a murderer.

Song of Solomon   Moussorgsky
I am the rose of Sharon, and the lily of the valley; as
the lily among thorns, so is my love among the daughters.   As the fair myrtle tree, amongst the barren trees
that wither in the forest, shineth my well beloved, midst
the hosts of lesser men, the youth of Israel.   Wherefore
hidest thou, my beloved?

Song of the flee   Moussorgsky
Long ago a king lived who kept a pet flea and cherished
him as dearly as a son.   He sent for his tailor and
clothed him in velvet, and gave him a jeweled order,
too! Ha! Ha! He made him a minister and gave him a
diamond to wear.   All of his relatives were given highest
orders.   Ha! Ha!   The courtiers were no longer gay,
for they were pestered by fleas, both night and day.
They were forbidden to scratch, no matter how much they
were bitten.   But we can scratch and kick when we are
bitten.   Ha! Ha!

Songs and Dances of Death   Moussorgsky
1. Trepắk
The forest and the banks of the river are desolate.   It is
a dark and windy night.   The country boy feels the embrace of Death, who holds him fondly and intones a song of
love and loneliness.   With the poor drunken man, he
dances to the Trepắk.   The wind blows, the tempest
rages.   Death, with his hypnotic song, lulls him into a
deep sleep.   He covers him.   The summer softly tiptoes
in, the flowers raise their little heads, and the doves
flutter about in the air.

2. Lullaby
The child hardly breathes and the mother at his side is in

despair. Death knocks at the door. "Do not be afraid,"
he says: "If you let me, I will put him to sleep with
tranquil dreams." The mother protests. She will not
give up her place near the small one's bed. It is her
sublime mission to keep her child warm. Death insists,
"I must speak to him so that he may sleep." And sleep
comes. "Do you see? He slept only because he heard
my lullaby."

3. Serenade
   The night is a deep blue, the dusk is tingling with life.
   The sick woman sees the beauty of the sky and listens
   to the silence which comes with the early morning. Under her window Death sings a serenade. He speaks of
   the youth which has passed her by and promises to free
   her from her suffering. He says he has been captivated
   by her flaming eyes, her warm breath, the enchantment
   of her rosy features, and calls her to the hour of promised ecstacy. "Come to my arms. Be still, you are
   mine."

4. Death, the Commander
   The battle rages. The cannons rumble through the dawn.
   The men fight without quarter and do not surrender.
   Night falls and the armies withdraw. On the battlefield
   remain only the dead and the wounded. Shrieks and
   groans are heard, and suddenly, Death arrives on horse-
   back, and his white hungry eyes survey the scene. He
   calls, "I have conquered you all. Life separated you,
   but Death will bring you together." They all rise at his
   beck in a silent parade, and descend down into the
   ground. "I stand sentinel that they will not return."

Sunless   Moussorgsky
1. Within four walls
   The little room is beautiful, peaceful and dark. Voices
   speak within my soul and my heart beats wildly. Swiftly
   and silently the moments fly. Dreams of happiness fade
   in the distance. All is uncertain, with no solution. She
   is my night, undescribable night.

2. You passed me unseen and unheeded
   You did not see nor heed me when you passed by. To
   me, your face was an unread riddle. Then you turned
   your head and I saw, in a moment, all the passion of
   years, the bliss of each love-filled moment, the tears,
   the oblivion, the sorrow.

3. The noisy day has sped its flight

The noisy day has sped its flight and now all is silent.
The darkness of a May night envelopes the city, but I,
burned by visions of daylight, cannot sleep. My heart
would rewrite the pages of past years. The poison of
a spring dream again stirs the hope, enchantment and
disillusionment of bygone days. I suffer on seeing these
phantoms, who speak an ancient language, but they do
not hold me. One vision arrests my gaze - my faithful
love of another time. For her I weep, blissfully and
tenderly.

4. You doll!
   You doll! It is your destiny to be a doll. Where is
   joy without passion? It is a return without absence, a
   victory without combat. Doll, you listen to words of passion with lying smiles and vacant heart. The path is always the same, from the cradle to the grave. We
   treasure life, but in death, peace comes to us.

5. Elegy
   The dark night sleeps while a solitary star twinkles in
   pale brilliance. Below, in the meadow, sadly sound the
   bells of grazing herds. Like nocturnal clouds, my way-
   ward thoughts surge within my heart, as images of despair. Dim hopes, once dear to me, have been long
   since lost, mingled with tears and regret. All around
   are darkest greed and poisonous lies from which there
   is no surcease. There is always the sound of the death
   knell. Oh bright star, you reach the shame of earth and
   there your image shines through the mist. Without you,
   my hopes would be lost in the shadows.

6. By the river
   The pale moon and stars of gold shine down on the
   waters below. I gaze at the lake's reflections, and mysteries, fanciful and sweet, creep into my soul. Boundless are the musings and dreams that enthrall me, as an
   ineffable voice soothes my heart. Sweet and cruel one,
   bid me to rest here.

The goat   Moussorgsky
A maiden walking through a field of flowers saw a goat.
It was old, dirty, evil and bearded. Terrified she fled
to the woods and hid.

The maiden went into the church and left with a husband.
He was aged, bald, evil and bearded. Do you think that
she fled from him? Oh no. She pretended that her love,
hm, was sent from above!

The Nursery   Moussorgsky
1. With Nanny
Tell me a story, Nanny, about the dreadful bogeyman
who ate naughty children, or about the king and queen
who lived across the sea in a splendid castle, or better
still tell me a funny tale!

2. In the corner
Nanny scolds the child and puts him in the corner for
scattering her knitting and spilling ink on it. He protests his innocence, saying the kitten was to blame for
the mischief. He calls Nanny a cross old thing - he
will not love her anymore.

3. The beetle
Nanny, hear what has happened. I built a house from
the prettiest twigs - a real house with a roof. A beetle
lighted on the roof and frightened me. He buzzed, spread
his wings, and struck me on the forehead. I was speechless, not daring to move. Then what did I see! He
was motionless, lying on his back, angry no more. Is
he dead, or is he feigning? Tell me, Nanny, what has
happened to him?

4. Dolly's cradle song
The little girl "mother" promises her doll a land filled
with oranges and candles if she will go to sleep.

5. Evening prayer
The child is breathless, remembering all the family in
his prayers. Suddenly he remembers that he has forgotten to mention himself.

6. The hobby horse
The little boy is riding his wooden horse over the vast
territories of his imagination. He meets his friend and
asks him to come and play in the evening. Soon the child
hurts himself and is comforted by his mother, who tells
him to be a brave little man. He is immediately all right.

7. Pussy cat
"Mother, I was looking for my sunshade when I saw our
little cat creep up to the bird cage. The bird was
trembling and chirping; I was angry! 'Puss, you'll kill
the birdy, will you?' Deceitfully he put his paw into the
cage. I hit him an awful blow. Mommy, are all bird
cages so hard? My fingers hurt very badly, how they
burn and tingle. Nasty pussy cat. Eh?"

The siege of Kazan, from "Boris Godounoff" Moussorgsky
The vagabond monk, Varlaam, bottle in hand, describes
the famous siege of Kazan. How the army of Czar Ivan
encompasses the Tatar city - the cannoniers, with
lighted fuse, set fire to the kegs of gunpowder and send
them hurtling into the stronghold of the enemy. How the
Tatars rend the air with awful shrieks and cries. Forty
thousand Tatars blown to pieces on that famous day!

MOZART
Mozart wrote about 35 songs, several of which are masterpieces, but his claim to fame, in vocal writing, lies
in his operas. He had a personal concept of opera as
an art. He had the ability to portray any character or
any situation, no matter how complicated. In his works
he can be extremely joyous, but there can also be sadness and tragedy. His talent for writing for the voice as
an instrument has probably been unsurpassed.

Abendempfindung (At evening) Mozart
The sun has set, and the moon casts down her silvery
glow. Thus do life's first hours go quickly by. Soon
the scene before us will be over, and the curtain fall;
then will our play be ended, and the tears of friendship,
shed over us, prove remembrance.

Ach, ich fühl's (Oh, I feel), from "Die Zauberflöte" Mozart
The "Magic Flute," an opera of fantasy and mystery,
somewhat in the same category as a Christmas panto-
mime, appealed strongly to Mozart's imagination and
called forth some of his most sublime music. Pamina,
who has been instructed by her mother, the Queen of the
Night, to kill the Highpriest Sarastro, finds Tamino indifferent to her attentions and only interested in his flute.
She bemoans her fate as she sings:

"Oh, I feel that all has vanished, the happiness of love
has flown from my heart. Forever banished are the
blissful hours I have known. Tamino, see my tears,
they flow alone for thee. If you do not feel the longing
of love, only death will give me rest."

Als Luise die Briefe (As Louise burned her love-letters)
Mozart
This song is sung as Luise burns the letters of her un-
true lover. "Perish, ye messengers of melancholy! The
hungry flames shall devour your songs, which were sung

not to me alone. Ye shall be burnt until no trace of
you remains - but ah! - your burning words will smoul-
der long within my heart!"

An Chloë (To Chloë)   Mozart
When love is shining in your blue, clear, truthful eyes,
when the joy of looking at them makes my heart beat and
glow, and I hold you and kiss your rosy cheeks, dearest
maiden, I tremble.   I embrace you, and press you to the
heart which leaves you only when it dies; a dark cloud
shades my drunken gazing and I sit quite spent, but happy,
next to you.

Aprite un po' quegl' occhi!   (Open your eyes a little bit)
from "Le Nozze di Figaro"   Mozart
The Countess and Susanna have played a joke on Figaro,
as well as on the Count.   Thinking that Susanna is unfaithful to him, Figaro bitterly sings: "All is ready, nor
can the moment for the revelation be far away.   O Susanna, to think that I am playing the role I used to mock
- the poor deceived husband.   To put faith in a woman
is folly.   Men, who take pride in your wives, open your
eyes.   See their tricks and their hearts that are as
false as their faces.   Like cats, they conceal their claws
and purr while waiting to trap their prey.

Batti, batti o bel Masetto (Scold me, dear Masetto), from
"Don Giovanni"   Mozart
In this scene, a wedding is in progress on the estate of
Don Giovanni.   He notices the charms of the bride and
makes love to her.   Masetto, her betrothed, does not
dare protest, as Don Giovanni significantly touches his
sword.   Later in the scene, the bride, Zerlina, in this
delightful aria, strives to make peace with Masetto.

Champagne Aria, from "Don Giovanni"   Mozart
Don Giovanni has joined a merry gathering of peasants,
singing and dancing, outside his palace gardens.   He
spots the pretty Zerlina among them and forthwith decides
to invite all to a feast in his palace.   "Let wine flow
like a fountain..."

Ch'io mi scordi di te (Am I forgotten?)   Mozart
Am I to be forgotten by one I know so well?   Why should
I want to live, I would rather die than know such life.
How can I survive new days of torment and grief.   Fear
not, beloved, my heart shall always be faithful.   Fatal
destiny and powers above will not soothe this suffering
heart.

Dalla sua pace (Upon her peace of mind), from "Don Giovanni" Mozart
My joy dependeth upon her peace of mind. Whatever she wishes, gives me life and what grieves her, gives me death. When she sighs, I also sigh and if fate does not smile at her, it does not smile at me.

Dans un bois (see: Einsam ging ich jüngst im Haine) Das Veilchen (The Violet) Mozart
A violet blossomed in a field, almost unseen. It was a beautiful violet. As the shepherdess came near the violet thought "I would I were the prettiest flower of all and my beloved would take me and carry me on her bosom." The maiden came and did not notice the beautiful little violet. She walked on and crushed it. It was a beautiful violet.

Deh vieni alla finestra (O come to the window), from "Don Giovanni" Mozart
This is Don Juan's Serenade which he sings to Donna Elvira. "Come to the window, my beloved, I sing to you of love. Come console my longing, else I die. Your lips are sweeter than honey and your breath as soft as the South wind. Come, my love, come to me."

Deh vieni non tardar (Come, do not delay), from "Le Nozze di Figaro" Mozart
Susanna and Figaro are to be married on the morrow but have quarreled. She comes into the rose garden and, knowing he is near, sings to him this lovely aria: "Come to me, my beloved. Do not delay, but come to me here by the roses."

Der Hölle Rache (Hell's revenge), from "Die Zauberflöte" Mozart
Hell's revenge boils in my heart, around me is death and despair. If you do not bring Sarastro the pangs of death, you are no more my daughter. Be disinherited for all eternity, cut for all times the filial bond. Listen, Gods of Revenge, listen to the mother's oath!

Dies Bildnis ist bezaubernd schön (This image is so beautiful), from "Die Zauberflöte" Mozart
This image is so beautiful that it makes my heart beat faster. Should this be love? Yes, love it is. Oh, would she be near! I would press her upon my heart and she would be mine forever.

Dove sono (Where are the happy moments), from "Le Nozze di Figaro" Mozart
Mozart's sparkling opera, "The Marriage of Figaro," was

founded on Beaumarchais' comedy, "Les Folies d'un
Jour," a sequel to "The Barber of Seville."

For a meeting with the Count, the Countess and her servant Susanna, the betrothed of Figaro, and also sought by
the Count, have planned to change clothes. Waiting for
Susanna, the Countess sings, "To what paltry tricks am
I driven by my husband's fault. Was ever lot so hard as
mine and so little deserved by me? A faithless husband,
yet jealous and suspicious, even while he betrays me!
Where are the happy moments! Have I lost him forever?
Can it be that love so ardent passes like a shadow, such
as clouds the summer-day? He again will love more
truly, since his heart has been astray."

Einsam ging ich jüngst im Haine (Lonely I walked in the
woods)   Mozart
As I walked in the lonely wood, I came to a little Cupid
sleeping. I sighed as I gazed. He awoke, and seizing
his avenging arrow, wounded me in the heart.

Il mio tesoro intanto (Console my beloved), from "Don Giovanni"   Mozart
Meanwhile go to my darling and console her. And from
her lovely lashes try to dry her teardrops. Tell her, I
will avenge her wrongs.

In diesen heil'gen Hallen (In these sacred halls), from "Die
Zauberflöte"   Mozart
"The Magic Flute" was written and produced in Vienna the
year of Mozart's death. In Act II of the opera, Tamino
and Papagano have been accepted as neophytes by Sarastro and the priests. They are left alone to undergo trials
to prove their worth when the Queen of Night appears to
tempt and frighten them. Sarastro re-enters and sings,
"In these sacred halls this wretch shall find rest. Soft
pity will heal his woes, friendship's hand shall stay his
steps and hope shall promise a better day. Fraternal
love and melancholy live here. Bid a willing pilgrim
share these joys."

L'amerò, sarò costante (I will love him forever), from "Il
Re Pastore"   Mozart
This aria, the only one for which this early opera is remembered, was a great favorite with Jenny Lind and with
Melba. The composer's beautiful melody provides a perfect opportunity for the display of vocal talents of colora-
turas. The double cadenza at the conclusion for voice

and instrument is an intricate and striking one.

Madamina, from "Don Giovanni"   Mozart
In Madamina, Leporello, servant of the most celebrated
lover of all time, catalogues with malicious glee the in-
numerable amorous adventures of his master, Don Giovanni, for the benefit of the latest victim, the unfortu-
nate Donna Elvira. The rascal Leporello enjoys the recital and the effect it creates, which gives a tragi-comic
character to the famous aria.

Mentre ti lascio (As I take leave of you)   Mozart
As I take leave of you, oh daughter, my heart trembles
within my breast. How bitter a parting! I depart...
you are weeping. Thus breaks my heart. Farewell.

Mi tradì quell'alma ingrata (Thou has betrayed me), from
"Don Giovanni"   Mozart
In what abyss of error have guilt and folly brought thee,
wretched Elvira! Wherefore is this longing? Cruel
heart, thou hast betrayed me, but love binds my heart
to him. Ne'er can I forget the past.

Non più andrai (You will go flirting no more), from "Le
Nozze di Figaro"   Mozart
This aria is sung by that sly rascal, Figaro, to the un-
fortunate Cherubino who is about to leave for foreign
lands in the Count's regiment. Figaro, in mock-heroic
manner, compares the gay and carefree life, which Cherubino has led so far, with what awaits him in the regiment.

Non so piu (I don't know), from "Le Nozze di Figaro"
Mozart
The part of Cherubino, the page of "The Marriage of Figaro," is always played by a soprano. He is most sus-
ceptible to the charms of women, and sings of his afflic-
tions in this brilliant aria: "I don't know what I'm doing
or saying. Every woman can set me aflutter and afire."

Non temer amato bene (Do not fear, beloved), from "Idomeneo"
Mozart
The Grand Heroic Opera, Idomeneo, centers around a
legendary tale of the King of Crete. The story was set
to music in 1712 by Andre Campra and was reworked in
1780 by Abbe Giambattista Varesco for Mozart's use. It
was first produced on January 29, 1781.

The whole work is conceived on a grand scale, and its

tragic force, the majesty of the choruses, and the brilliance of the orchestration give it a unique place among the composer's works.

O Isis und Osiris, from "Die Zauberflöte"   Mozart
O Isis and Osiris, give wisdom to the united lovers!
Strengthen them with patience in danger, but should they go to their grave, guide them to your dwelling.

Oiseaux, si tous les ans (Birds, every year)   Mozart
Birds, every year you change your climates. As soon as winter comes, you fly away because your destiny does not permit you to love except when the flowers bloom. When the season is gone, you go elsewhere to find love so that you may love the whole year round.

Osmin's Aria from "Die Entführung aus dem Seraglio" Mozart
The story of the opera is concerned with the loves of Constance and Belmont and their adventures after they are captured by Corsairs and sold as slaves to the Turks. This song of triumph is sung by the Pasha's overseer, Osmin, as he catches the lovers - just as they are about to escape from the harem.

Parto, parto! (I leave), from "Titus"   Mozart
I will fly to avenge you, my dear love. I will be all that pleases you; all that you desire, I will do. Grant me one loving glance and all else disappears, Oh, gods! What power you have given to beauty.

Porgi amor (Love, relieve my suffering), from "Le Nozze di Figaro"   Mozart
Love, relieve my suffering, give me back my beloved or let me die.

Rivolgete a lui lo sguardo (Turn your eyes to him)   Mozart
This piece, intended to be included in "Così fan tutte," was composed in December 1789, before the opera was finished. For this number Mozart had the baritone Benucci in mind, who sang later the part of Guglielmo in the first performance.

Guglielmo and Ferrando are trying, on a wager with Don Alfonso, each to win the affection of the other's betrothed. In the guise of a rich Albanian, Guglielmo tries hard to melt Dorabella's heart, and also to help the fictitious suit of his friend:

"Turn your eyes toward him and you will see what he

feels. He says: I freeze. I burn...My idol, have pity! and for just a moment, my dear, direct your beautiful eyes towards me and you will see in mine what my lips cannot express. Enamored Roland cannot compare with me. The wounded breast of a Medor is as nothing, compared to mine. My sighs are of fire, my desires as strong as bronze. If then one speaks of merit, I am sure (and so is he) that our equal cannot be found from Vienna to Canada. In wealth we are like Croesus, in beauty like Narcissus, in love, even Mark Antony would seem ridiculous compared to us. We are stronger than a Cyclops, as men of learning we are equal to Aesop. If we dance, a Puck would give up, so delicate and fleet are our feet. If we sing, with a single trill we would outshine the nightingale. And some other talents have we too, that no one knows. -- (Aside) Splendid, splendid, they resist us firmly. They are leaving, and I am glad of it. Models of loyalty, they are paragons of faithfulness!"

Se vuol ballare (If you want to dance), from "Le Nozze di Figaro"   Mozart
The plot of "The Marriage of Figaro" is a continuation of "The Barber of Seville." Rosina and the Count Almaviva have been married, and now arrangements are being made for the wedding of Figaro and Susanna, the countess' maid. The count, none too true to Rosina, bothers Susanna with his attentions. She advises Figaro of this and he plans to embarrass the count. In this aria he tells of his plans: "I'll play the tune for my lord, if he wants to dance. He can dance at his leisure while I slyly plan and maneuver frustrating schemes."

Sehnsucht nach dem Frühling (Longing for spring)   Mozart
Come, sweet May, and cover the trees again with green. Let me see little violets blooming by the river's brim. 'Tis true that winter days have their delights; but spring is milder and greener outside! Come, sweet May, and bring violets, nightingales and cuckoos with thee.

Trio: Farewell scene, from "Die Zauberflötte"   Mozart
The priests, with Sarastro, have again assembled in the temple to discuss the two lovers, Pamina and Tamino. When they are brought in, Sarastro tells them to bid each other farewell, with the assurance that Tamino will endure to the end of his trials and that they will soon meet in joy.

Un' aura amorosa (A gentle breeze), from "Cosi fan tutte" Mozart

Gentle breeze around our beloved, sweetly restore the heart. The heart which is nourished by hope of love, does not need a better bait.

Un moto di gioia (An excitement of Joy)   Mozart
Three years after Mozart composed "The Marriage of Figaro," he wrote this short arietta as a substitute for the more familiar "Deh vieni non tardar," so it appears only in the Appendix to the opera.

My heart is bounding with pleasure, and sorrow turns into joy. Hope's gentle whispers have given solace. Not always is grief a part of love.

Voi che sapete (You who know), from "Le Nozze di Figaro" Mozart
You, who understand love, must know whether love is in my heart. I am constantly changing from hot to cold and I find peace in neither night nor day.

Warnung (Warning)   Mozart
Men are always fond of flirting. Beware, pretty maids! Fathers, keep your daughters safe at home!

NIN
Joaquin Nin y Castellano was a native of Cuba. He was born in Havana, September 9th, 1883, but studied at Barcelona and Paris and lived mostly in the latter city, apart from his numerous concert tours. He saturated himself with Spanish music, especially folksong and eighteenth century classics. His works include arrangements of folktunes and a Spanish Suite.

El amor es como un nino (Love is like a baby)   Nin
Love is like a baby, capricious and whimsical. It takes a spoon, gets hurt and cries. There is no love equal to mine, in spite of your cruelty, oh, tyrant of my life. Can I give more? My love is unchangeable.

El vito (The life)   Nin
Popular song of Madrid, 1800. "An old one is worth a dime and a young one two quarters, but I, being poor, dance with the cheaper."

Granadina   Nin
The effort of loving is the greatest of efforts because one cries, in singing, yet the tears do not come. Strike me with this dagger and you will say that you have killed me, and, in the color of the blood, you will see that I love you.

Malagueña   Nin
Even my horse wept, when I left Marbella, because I
left my beloved one who reflects the sunshine.

Al amor (To love)   Obradors
Give me numberless kisses, then hundreds, thousands
and millions more. And as nobody pays attention, we
stop adding and count back.

Coplas de curro dulce (Song of a tender fellow)   Obradors
"Ah! the tiny little bride, the tiny little groom, the tiny
little parlor and the tiny little room. That is why the
resting-place must be very, very small as well as the
mosquito netting."

Corazón, por qué pasais (Heart, why do you pass)   Obradors
My heart, why do you pass the night of love in vigil,
when your master rests in the arms of another?

Del cabello mas sutil (Of the finest hair)   Obradors
I want to make a chain of the finest hair in your braids,
to tie you to me. I would like to be a little jug in your
home so that I might kiss your lips each time you take
a drink.

El vito (The life)   arr. Obradors
Popular song of Madrid - 1800.
An old one is worth a dime and a young one two quarters,
but I, being poor, dance with the cheaper.

La mi sola Laureola (My only Laureola)   Obradors
"My only Laureola," the captivated Leriano says, "although
my pride is wounded by thy hand, it is the only hand in
the world for me !"

Tres morillas (Three brunettes)   Obradors
I am in love with three brunettes. They went to gather
olives...They went to gather them and returned palid and
tired...Three lovely brunettes went to gather apples.

Tumba y lé   Obradors
Though but a maiden, if by chance I take a husband, each
year I shall bear his children till they are countless!
Come along - enjoy life e'er it fleets to tranquil ways -
come along and play for soon I go to my chores.

Barcarolle, from "Les Contes d'Hoffman"   Offenbach
Offenbach (1819-1880) is the creator of French burlesque
opera. His works were all the rage under the Second

95

Empire and many are still played in Paris and elsewhere.

The fanciful imagination of Hoffman's Tales found a perfect complement in the music of Jacques Offenbach, and this fantastic opera is now ranked as the composer's masterpiece.
"Beautiful night, smile on us lovers! Beautiful night, sweeter than day - time for love!"

Les l'oiseaux dans la charmille (All the birds in every tree), from "Les Contes d'Hoffmann" Offenbach
All the birds, in every tree, and every ray of the sun, sing to me of love. All creatures that sing move me to trembling and sighing of love. Oh, hear Olympia's love-song.

Scintille, diamant (Shine, diamond), from "Les Contes d'Hoffmann" Offenbach
The magician, Dapertutto, holds in his sway the beautiful courtesan, Giulietta; for him, she has stolen the shadow of her lover, Schlemil, and now he wishes her to ensnare Hoffman in order to steal his reflection in a mirror.
'Mirror, where the lark is ensnared, draw her to you. Be she lark or woman, she is caught in your spell. One loses her life to you, and the other her soul..."

Tu n'est pas beau (You are not handsome), from "La Périchole" Offenbach
You have no looks nor wealth, you lack a brilliant sort of mind, and you behave most oddly. You show not a trace of talent to make you pleasing! You are slow and you know you're a rascal. Yet, I adore you and will love you alone till I die!

Princesita (Little princess) Padilla
Little Princess, with eyes of blue and lips of red. You are like a butterfly of beautiful colors. Kiss me! Kiss me!

Chi vuol la zingarella (Who wants the gypsy) Paisiello
Who wants the gypsy woman, beautiful and bright? Here she is. I know how to guess women's futures and how to intrigue men.

Nel cor più non mi sento (I feel nothing in my heart) from "La Molinara" Paisiello
Why does my heart feel so dormant, with no fire of youth? You, O love, are the cause of my torment, the

fault is yours!

Psyché Paladilhe
   I am jealous of all nature, Psyché! The sunbeams are
   kissing you, the wind caresses your hair. Even the air
   you inhale touches your lips and your dress clings to
   you! And when you sigh - I am afraid.

Quel ruscelletto (The brooklet)   Paradies
   The sprightly music of this song pictures the brooklet
   in its restless course, babbling the secret confided to it
   by a poet about his love for a fair maiden.

Al tramontar del giorno (At sunset)   Pasquini
   As in the setting sun, all nature seems to go to slumber,
   and as the beauty of the rose dims after days of radiance, so will human beauty fade at the sunset of life...

Quanto è folle (How silly it is)   Pasquini
   How silly it is for a lover to despair of inconstant and
   everchanging fortune. The longing for pity is common to
   lovers, so I pledge my eternal constancy to my beloved
   Chloris!

So ben s'io peno (I know I suffer)   Pasquini
   I know I suffer though hope still lives in my breast. My
   heart is torn with fear. I tremble. I know what it is
   to suffer! I know that death is near, yet I still have
   faith; I am at last serene. I know what it is to suffer.

Mentre dormi, Amor fomenti (While you are sleeping, Amor),
from "Olimpiade" Pergolesi
   While you are sleeping, Amor, multiply the joy of your
   dreams with the thought of my joy. The brooklet should
   flow slowly and the zephyr should stop its murmuring.

Nina   Pergolesi
   For three days my Nina has lain upon her bed. Pipes,
   drums and cymbals, awake my Ninetta that she may sleep
   no more.

Se tu m'ami (If you love me)   Pergolesi
   If you love me, if you sigh for me, gentle shepherd, I
   feel sorry for you because I know you will be disap-
   pointed.

Stizzoso, mio stizzoso (My angry one), from "La Serva Pa-
drona"   Pergolesi
   My angry one, you are very conceited. I will not help

97

you for you are obliged to obey me. Stay quiet and do not talk, Serpina wishes it that way.

Gioite al canto mio (Rejoice to my singing), from "Euridice" Peri
  The Florentine Camerata attempting to prove that Greek drama had been accompanied by music, commissioned Peri and the author, Rinnuccini, to write the opera "Euridice." Thus, the earliest opera came into being. The opera was also included in the marriage festivities of Henry IV, of France, and Maria de Medici. This aria is the invocation of Orpheus to the light as he returns from the underworld.

  Rejoice to my singing, verdant hills and hidden valleys. The Sun is revived and adorned with bright eyes which put Delos to shame. She lights the day and, in kindling the fire within souls, enslaves Earth and Heaven to Love.

Rosemonde Persico
  Once upon a time there was a garden in which I saw fair Rosemonde. Lovely birds floated in the air while a gentle shade settled over the woods. Once upon a time there was a spring and I drank there with Rosemonde. Some Naiads passed and I watched the ripple of pearls at their fingertips. Once upon a time I gave a kiss to Rosemonde. "Look! Two kisses!" said a blond nymph. "No," said the other, "there were three!" Once upon a time there was a flower which came from the heart of Rosemonde. It is my soul and I languish. In the deep of night I hear the singing of voices.

Dolce, scherza (Sweetly play) Perti
  O lips, which inspire my love, sweetly play and sweetly laugh. Yet they entice and destroy me thus afflicting the heart.

Requiem du coeur (Requiem of the heart) Pessard
  My heart is dead. I tied it within its bier this morning and threw the key to the bottom of the river. Fill my glass! Tra - la - la!

O nuit, déesse du mystère (O Night, mysterious goddess)
Piccini
  O Night, mysterious goddess, love's dear companion and friend, hasten, that day may end. I sigh, I tremble, I languish with hope and with despair.

En barque (In a bark) Pierné

Stay awhile, mignonne, let us enjoy the fleeting moments of love's ecstasy as we float over the quiet, rippling water.

Ils étaient trois petits chats blancs (Three little white cats) Pierné
A back-yard epic about "three little white cats."

I pastori (The shepherds)   Pizzetti
Shepherds, migrating from the Abruzzi to the Adriatic, pass beautiful scenes. There are green meadows, the wild sea, the fruits of the filbert tree, the ancient trails and the sounds of sheep..."Ah, why am I not with my shepherds !"

Dansons la gigue (Let us dance the jig)   Poldowski
Lady Dean Paul, whose nom de plume was Poldowski, was the daughter of the famous Polish violinist, Wieniawski. She composed a number of songs. A great admirer of the French poet, Paul Verlaine, she set sixteen of his lyrics to music.

Cielo e mar (Heaven and ocean), from "La Giocanda"   Ponchielli
Over heaven and ocean an ethereal veil shines like a holy altar. Will my angel come from the sky or from the sea? Here I await her as the zephir speaks of love. In the melting breeze neither earth nor mountains appear, only the horizon kisses the waves. Come, my lady, for the kiss of life and love.

Suicidio! (Yes, suicide), from "La Gioconda"   Ponchielli
Only suicide is left for me. I have no other hope. I have lost my mother and my lover is dying. Conquered by jealousy, I sink, exhausted, to the grave.

Voce di donna o d'angelo (Oh blessed and angelic voice), from "La Gioconda"   Ponchielli
Oh, blessed and angelic one, be merciful and illumine my blind eyes. Ah! No! I will give you this rosary with all of its prayers. It will watch over you and bless you in the future.

POULENC
Poulenc is one of the leading composers in French music today. He revealed unusual musical ability as a boy, was a pupil of Vines and Koechlin, and achieved fame as one of the members of the famous group of advanced young French composers. He has composed in various

99

forms; much of his work is in the style that seeks to capture a neo-classic transparency and delicacy of texture; he is often deliberately simple and melodious. There is a free, melodic abundance in his finished works and he possesses a rare sense of tone values.

Airs Chantés   Poulenc
1. Air romantique (Romantic song)
   I wandered through the countryside, although the storm and wind defied me. The clouds hung low in the dark morning and a black raven seemed to guide me through the pools of the driven rain. The lightning flashed in splendor and the groaning wind grew louder. My heart was beating in a vague terror, stronger than the storm. The autumn gathered the golden leaves and the raven flew with me to my destination.

2. Air champêtre (Country song)
   Beautiful brooklet, I always remember how I was once led to you in friendship. I gaze into the radiant features of a goddess half lost in the moss and sedge of the shore. Oh nymph, I long to follow you, enslaved. Oh, that I might mingle with the breeze and reply to the hidden wave.

3. Air grave (Song of grief)
   Depart from my mind, angry thoughts of pain, remorse and disgrace. Go, cruel memories, that hold my brain in death-like embrace. Moss covered paths, playing fountains, rocky caverns, songs of birds and wind, dim shadows of the beasts of the forest, do not spurn and reject me. Oh, Nature, that gives gladness, hear me when I cry! Hide the remorse and disgrace in my soul.

4. Air vif (Brisk song)
   The orchard is white, the countryside is rejoicing, - the meadows and groves, bursting into bloom, listen to the voice of the wind that sighs above. Serene ocean, even though storms rage and awaken your sorrow, you are never shaken and calmly repose.

A sa guitare (To his guitar)   Poulenc
   I sing to my guitar of the loves I have received. The sounds of its harmonies will cool the eternal flame of my longing.

Attributs (Tribute)   Poulenc
   To the Gods and Goddesses of legend belong the good things of the earth. Cares and tears are sacred only to

the Goddess, Cytherea.

Avant le cinema (At the cinema)   Poulenc
Tonight we go to the cinema. Who are the artists?
They are not those who cultivate the fine arts - art, poetic art or music; they are the actors and actresses.
If we were artists, we would say cine, not cinema. If
we were old professors from the provinces, we would
say neither cine nor cinema, but cinematograph. You
understand, we must have good taste!

Bleuet (Cornflower)   Poulenc
Young man of 20 years, who has seen such tragic things,
what do you know of the men of your childhood? You
know bravery and ruse, you have been face to face with
Death one hundred times - but you do not know what
Life is, because you know more of Death than Life.

Chanson d'Orkenise (Song of Orkenise)   Poulenc
A cart-driver wishes to pass through the gates of Orkenise, but the guards ask him what he is bringing to the
city. He answers, he brings only his heart, so that he
can marry. At the same time a beggar leaves through
the gates. The guards ask him what he has taken from
the city, and he answers, he has left his heart there.
How many hearts are in Orkenise! The guards laugh.
The beggar's path is cruel, but love is also cruel. O
cart-driver. The handsome guards of the city parade
superbly in front of the gates, which close slowly.

Chanson du clair tamis (The flower sifter's song)   Poulenc
The church warden will pass through the poppies where
the emblem bearer has passed. The Bishop's representative is dead, killed by pretty eyes. Let us cry over his
happy fate, buried with the cross of Lorraine on his
jacket and with his sword under him.

A bird in the branches sings, "coo-coo." Tomorrow is
Sunday and a feast day for our villagers. There will be
the clarinet, low sounding trombones, light wines and
bagpipes. The elders will be the drunkest and grand-
mother, with her bell-shaped glasses, will be on her
young legs. Comes the spring, pretty one, where the
frog has passed over the buttercups, and the beetle will
pass.

Chansons Gaillards (Merry Songs)   Poulenc
1. La maîtraisse volage (The fickle mistress)
My mistress is fickle, my rival is happy; if he has a

bag of fleas, she certainly has two. He rows the boat -
she can too!

2. Chanson à boire (Drinking song)
   The kings of Egypt and of Syria wanted their bodies to be
   embalmed, to last much longer - dead. What folly,
   let's drink again. Then let's drink all our life long and
   be embalmed before death. How sweet it is to embalm
   ourselves.

3. Madrigal
   You are beautiful like an angel, gentle like a tiny lamb.
   But there is no heart in your feelings, Jeannette, and a
   girl without a breast is like a partridge without oranges.

4. Invocation aux Parques (Invocation to Fate)
   I swear as long as I live to love you, Sylvia. Fate,
   which in its hand is holding the thread of our life, pro-
   long mine as long as you can, I beg you.

5. Couplets bachiques (Verses of a drunkard)
   As long as the day lasts, I am grave or merry. If I see
   a flask without wine, I am sad - if it is full, I am happy.
   When my wife keeps me in bed, I am wise the whole
   night long. If another shares my bed, I am playful. Ah!
   beautiful hostess, pour me some wine.

6. L'offrande (The offering)
   To the God of love, a maiden offered a candle to obtain
   a lover. The God smiled at her demand and said to her:
   "Beautiful one, whilst waiting, cherish the candle - ha!"

7. La belle jeunesse (The handsome youth)
   One must always love and never marry. Gentlemen,
   stop being marrying men, aim at "tirelires" and "tourelours," don't aim at their hearts. Why marry if the
   wives of others do not have to be asked to be ours. Because their ardors and their favors are only looking for
   our "tirelires" and "tourelours" and our hearts.

8. Sérénade (Serenade)
   With such a beautiful hand, which is used with so much
   charm, you should obtain the weapons from Amor. And
   if the "little god" turns unhappy - dry his tears.

Hôtel   Poulenc
   My room is like a cage. The sun thrusts his arm through
   my window, but I - I just wish to smoke. I do not wish
   to work or walk, just smoke my cigarette.

Le Bestiare (The Beasts)   Poulenc
1. Le dromadaire (The dromedary)
   With his four dromedaries, Don Pedro d'Alfarou went to
   see the world. That is what I should like to do, if I
   had four dromedaries.

2. La chèvre du Thibet (The goat from Tibet)
   The fleece of this goat, or even the golden fleece of the
   one for which Jason went to such trouble, is not worth
   as much as the hair of my beloved.

3. La sauterelle (The grasshopper)
   Here is the slender grasshopper, the nourishment of
   Saint John. Would that my verses could be, like the
   grasshopper, a feast for the best people.

4. Le dauphin (The dolphin)
   Dolphins, you play in the sea, but the wave is always bitter.
   Sometimes my joy burst out, but life is rather cruel.

5. L'écrevisse (The crab)
   Uncertainty, o my delight!   You and I go together, just
   as the crabs do - backwards, backwards.

6. La carpe (The carp)
   In your ponds, in your pools, carp, how long you live!
   Has death forgotten you, fish of melancholy?

Les ponts de C (The bridges of C)   Poulenc
   "C" is a village built on the islands formed by several
   branches of the Loire River. There, in 1940, a French
   army attempted in vain to stop the invasion. The poet,
   Louis Aragon, evokes gallant memories of the "Chateaux
   de la Loire" while crossing the bridges with the defeated
   army.

Montparnasse   Poulenc
   O door of the hotel, with two green plants, green which
   will never bear flowers, where are my fruits? Where
   did I plant myself? O door of the hotel, an angel is before you, distributing leaflets. Virtue has never been
   well rewarded. Give me, forever, a room by the week.
   Bearded angel, you are in reality a lyric poet from Germany who wished to know Paris. You know, from its
   streets, those lines over which one must not walk, and
   you dream of spending your Sunday in the suburbs. The
   weather is a little heavy and your hair is long.

   O good little poet, a little silly and with hair too blond,

your eyes resemble so much these two large balloons
which are rising at random in the pure air.

Priez pour paix (Pray for peace)   Poulenc
Pray for Peace, sweet Mary. Ask your Son to show
His people that He wished to abolish all wars by His
sorrows. Pray for Peace, the real treasure of joy.

La strada bianca (The white road)   Pratella
Go on, walk, walk...the short road ends. Here starts
the white road, oh my beloved. You will continue without stopping, without listening to me, without seeing me
anymore. After my death turn your face to me that I
may see your departure. This is forever, my sweet child
...until the stars of the white road, until our death.
Go on, go on...

Snowdrop-tree   Prokofieff
There is a blooming snowdrop-tree. Raspberries grow
in the dale. A fair lass climbed up the hill and she
picked some blossoms there. Ah!

Snowflakes   Prokofieff
Fields and meadows are all sleeping, soft snowflakes
have covered them. But my woestruck heart is bleeding
and my pain remains the same. Days are dull, nights
dark and hopeless, tears running down my cheeks. Snow
is melting where a tear drops, and green grass begins
to grow.

PUCCINI
Puccini was the greatest of the post-Verdi Italian opera
composers. His extremely popular operas are based on
openly sentimental vocal lines and orchestral treatment,
and give ample opportunity for vocal display in melodramatic situations. His operas are characterized by
throbbing climaxes and an exceptional ability to delineate
heroes and heroines. ·

Che gelida manina (How cold your little hand is), from "La
Bohème"   Puccini
How cold your little hand is! Let me warm it while I
tell you about myself and my profession. I am a poet
and I write. How do I live? Somehow! In my poverty
I dream of richness and castles and write love poems.
And now, two beautiful eyes have stolen all my imagined
treasures. But I don't mind, as they bring new hope!
Now you know who I am, please tell me about yourself.

Donna, non vidi mai (Never have I seen a lovelier woman),
from "Manon Lescaut"   Puccini
Never have I seen a lovelier woman. To tell her my
love would awaken new life in my soul. I hear her
voice, "Manon Lescaut I'm called." How her name stirs
my spirit and hidden thoughts caress me. Oh, gentle
whispering, do not end.

Duet: **O soave fanciulla** (O gentle maiden), from "La
Bohème"   Puccini
The scene of La Bohème is laid in the Latin Quarter of
Paris. Rudolph, a struggling poet sharing an attic with
three other Bohemians, has just burned his manuscripts
in an effort to warm the cold room. They have gathered
enough money to pay their rent, but have decided to
spend it for a revel instead. Rudolph's three friends
start out for the Quarter's cafes, but Rudolph remains
to work. He is soon interrupted by Mimi, a pretty neigh-
bor, who comes in to re-light her candle which has gone
out on the stairs. She drops her key and Rudolph re-
trieves it during the search without telling her he has
found it. The visit, thus prolonged, gives them opportunity for conversation. They each tell the other about
themselves, and finally reveal their love for one another
in this duet.

E lucevan le stelle (The stars were shining), from "Tosca"
Puccini
The stars were shining and the air full of perfumes.
She came to me in the garden and took me in her arms.
What sweet kisses and tender caresses! Gone forever
is the dream of love and I die in despair! And never
had I loved life so much.

In quelle trine morbide (In those soft laces), from "Manon
Lescaut"   Puccini
Manon, whose great beauty and love of luxury eventually
prove her undoing, confesses boredom with her rich surroundings and her great longing for the man she really
loves.

"In the soft, lace curtains of this gilded spot there is
silence and a freezing chill. I once knew the ardor of
passionate kisses, but now all is gone. Oh my humble
abode, you appear before my eyes as a vision - full of
joy, secluded and white - a gentle dream of peace and of
love."

Mi chiamano Mimi (They call me Mimi), from "La Bohème"
Puccini

They call me Mimi, but my name is Lucia. I embroider
and make flowers, which speak to me of love and of
springtime. I live alone in an attic where the first rays
of the springtime sun are mine. I dearly love real
roses, for the ones I make have no fragrance. That is
all there is to tell you of myself.

Nessun dorma! (No one must sleep), from "Turandot"
Puccini

No one must sleep. O Princess, you look from your
window to the night where the stars tremble with love.
The mystery of my name is locked within my breast, but
on the morrow, with a kiss, I will break the silence and
you will be mine forever.

O mio babbino caro (O my beloved daddy), from 'Gianni
Schicchi" Puccini

O my beloved daddy, I love him as my King. I'm going
to buy our wedding ring at the Porta Rossa. If you still
say no, I'll throw myself from the Ponte Vecchio. Suffering and languishing, I want to die. Daddy, I pray, let
me buy the ring.

Quando me'n vo' (When they see me), from "La Bohème"
Puccini

With little success, Musetta and Marcel attempt to appear
indifferent to each other when they meet at the Cafe Mo-
mus. Then, Musetta, without arousing the suspicion of
her aged escort, boldly and deliberately sings a light,
airy waltz to Marcel to make him aware of her love for
him.

Recondita armonia (Strange harmony), from "Tosca" Puccini

Cavaradossi, painting a blue eyed Madonna in the church,
has used an unknown worshiper as a model. He sings of
her beauty and the harmony of her features.

Tu che di gel sei cinta (You, who in ice are girded), from
"Turandot" Puccini

You, girded in ice, vanquished by fire, will also love
him! My tired eyes shall close before the dawn so that
victory may once again be his. In death I will repose!

Un bel dì vedremo (One fine day we will see), from 'Madama
Butterfly" Puccini

The scene is the interior of Butterfly's home, where the
childlike bride gives expression to the beautiful hope and

strong faith she has in the eventual return of her American husband.

One fine day we will see a wisp of smoke on the horizon. The cannons will roar and I will go to meet him. Do you know what he'll say when he comes to where I will be waiting on the hill? He will call, "Butterfly," but I will hide quietly - to tease him and to not die at our first meeting. He will then call me the other names he used to call me. Banish your fears, Suzuki, he will return! I know it!

Vissi d'arte, vissi d'amore (I lived for art and for love), from "Tosca"   Puccini
I lived for art and for love and never harmed anyone! In sincere faith I prayed to the Lord and laid flowers on the altar. I gave jewels to adorn the Madonna and my songs greeted the stars in heaven. Why, Lord, hast Thou forsaken me in this hour of suffering?

Man is for the woman made   Purcell
The contemporary historian, P.H. Lang, records that critics of Purcell's church music considered him too "happy" and "irreverent." The true greatness of his musical stature is attested to by the fact that two of his works so impressed the "critical cantor of St. Thomas's" that J.S.B. copied them into his handbook. Until recent times the Bach Society thought them original works of the great German master.

Tes yeux (Your eyes)   Rabey
Your lovely eyes pour the warmth of your desire into my heart. They burn like fire and kindle the glow of divine love in my breast. Their radiance dispels the lightest care of the shadows that rise like clouds. Your beautiful eyes, that look so deep and true, pour into my heart the warmth of your desire. They shall be my guiding stars throughout my life.

RACHMANINOFF
Rachmaninoff, one of the greatest virtuosi pianists of his time, was a noted composer of Russian song. His first big success as a composer was the opera "Aleko," which won for him the Gold Medal Prize upon his graduation from the Moscow Conservatory. His 68 songs are best described as being spontaneous and inspired, built on a fine lyric declamation, long and spacious phrases and sweeping accompaniments.

All things depart   Rachmaninoff
All things depart, nothing remains. Life rushes on like
fleeting time. A flower blooms, but its petals soon are
withered. The glowing flame soon ceases to burn.
Soon will the ecstasy of my song fade away.

Before my window   Rachmaninoff
Before my window a cherry-tree is in bloom. Lost in
rapture, I breathe its perfumed blossoms until their
heady sweetness sets my senses reeling...The cherry
blossoms sing to me their tender song.

Christ is risen   Rachmaninoff
The choirs sing, "Christ is risen," but my soul is sad.
The earth is still dark with strife and tears, even as the
hymn is sung. O Virgin Mother, if Thou wert reborn
and could see the hate of man, Thy tears would flow upon hearing the chant, "Christ is risen."

Excerpt from Musset   Rachmaninoff
Why is my heart beating so fast? Am I expecting some-
body? Did someone come in? Oh no, it is midnight.
My lonely cell is empty. I am alone. Ah, despair.

Floods of spring   Rachmaninoff
The fields are still covered by snow, but the waters are
already announcing the Spring. She sends us out to an-
nounce her arrival.

How sweet the place   Rachmaninoff
How sweet the place! Far distant gleams the river in
the sun; the grassy meadows at my feet are overrun with
flowers. No one is near but God and I, the distant
peaceful stream, this lonely pine, the host of flowers,
and you, my lovely dream.

In the silence of night   Rachmaninoff
Oh, in the silent night, I still can hear your bitter,
cruel words and feel your glance. The beauty of your
smile languishes but soon commands. I recall the vague
and troubled thoughts and the murmured promises which
were broken. Rapture enflames my being and I cry a-
loud. With longing heart I cry that night may know your
name.

Lilacs   Rachmaninoff
The sun rises upon the blooming lilac trees and I inhale
the fresh morning air. I wander in search of happiness
in the cool shade. Only a few people find the joy they

seek, mine is where the lilacs bloom.

Oh, cease thy singing, maiden fair   Rachmaninoff
Fair maiden, cease your singing of Georgian lands. Banish those thoughts of our life in foreign lands.   Your
haunting memories recall the moon, the desert night and
imploring eyes.

Oh no, I pray, do not depart!   Rachmaninoff
Oh no, I pray, do not depart!   I am too happy for the
anguish of farewell.   Oh say, "I love." I need you very
much, for new torments will assail my heart.   Oh stay
with me, do not depart!

O thou billowy harvest-field   Rachmaninoff
O billowy harvest-field of grain, may you never be
mown, may your sheaves never be bound. Oh thoughts
and dreams filled with care, who can gather you, who
can bind you into words!

Serenade of the Gypsy Boy, from "Aleko"   Rachmaninoff
In addition to being one of the world's great pianists,
conductors and composers, Rachmaninoff was a master
of writing songs. He belonged to the old school where
melody was of paramount importance, and this is illus-
trated in his songs.

Look at the moon! She covers the immense world with
her light. Who has the courage to tell the moon to stop
and to not move? Who can tell a heart to be faithful?

The island   Rachmaninoff
A little island, to protect itself, grew roses, violets, and
laurel trees around its shores. The quiet waters reflect
majestic and beautiful images, and as in a dream, the
island sleeps like a child.

To the children   Rachmaninoff
How often, at night, have I watched you, blessed you with
the sign of the Cross and prayed the Almighty to protect
you. Now all is quiet in the nursery; you have become
adults and gone into the world. Dear children, now
pray for the one who prayed for you and blessed you with
the sign of the Cross.

Vocalise (Song without words)   Rachmaninoff

Puissant maître des flots (Mighty Lord of the deep), from
'Hippolyte et Aricie" Rameau
Mighty Lord of the deep, Neptune listen to the trembling
cry of thy son. Hear Thou his last lament.

En gammal dansrytm (An old dance rhythm) Rangström
As we two are dancing, torn with burning passion and
fiery love, earth melts to ashes under our feet. We
dance in ecstasy! Dance!!

RAVEL
Ravel is known as a neoclassic composer. His melodic
line has a conversational tone, his sonorities are strange
and colorful, and his musical forms are characterized
by his fondness for the dance. He liked the archaic and,
in his compositions, discarded the superficial. Many of
his songs are a delight of sophisticated humor and wit,
and have a Spanish color which can be traced to the influence of his boyhood near the Spanish border.

Air du Feu (Song of the Fire), from "L'Enfant et les
Sortilèges"
The Fairy has disappeared, the child is left alone. "Thou,
heart of the rose, perfume of the lily, art gone, leaving
only a strand of the golden hair on my shoulder - and a
shattered dream."

Aria of the Fire, from "L'Enfant et les Sortilèges" Ravel
Away, child! I warm the good but I burn the wicked.
Beware little savage, you have insulted the Gods who
hold the fate of fortune or misfortune. You have upset
the kettle and scattered the matches. Beware of fire,
you will melt like a snow-flake.

Cinq Melodies Populaires Grecques Ravel
1. Chanson de la mariée (Song of the bride)
Wake up, my dear! It's morning!

2. Là-bas, vers l'église (Over there, towards the church)
Over there, where the church tower of Ayio Sidero
shines, the pious and faithful of the world have come.

3. Quel galant (Which gallant)
Which gallant can compare with me? Tell me, Madame
Vasiliki! See my sword, my pistols and my saber --
and it's you I love.

4. Chanson des cueilleuses de lentisques (Song of the lentisk
gatherers)

Ah, my best beloved, my heart's treasure, my dearest
one, when thou art near, then alas, am I worn with
sighing.

5. Tout gai! (Be gay!)
   Be gay, Love, be gay!

Deux Mélodies Hébraïques (Two Hebrew melodies)   Ravel
1. Kaddisch (Prayer)
   Thy glory be praised, O King of Kings, Thou who changes
   the world and who revives the dead.   Thy Kingdom, O
   Lord, be proclaimed for us, the children of Israel, today, tomorrow and always. Let us say: "Amen." Thy
   name be loved and cherished and Thy name be glori-
   fied.

2. L'énigma éternelle (The eternal enigma)
   To the questions of the world, one answers tra la la if
   one cannot answer.   Tra la la.

Don Quichotte À Dulcinée (Don Quixote To Dulcinea)   Ravel
1. Chanson romanesque (Romantic song)
   If you were to tell me that the earth, in turning, of-
   fended you, I would send off Panza, and you would see it
   motionless. If you were to tell me that the sky was too
   full of stars, with one blow I would rip apart the heavens.
   But were you to tell me that my blood belonged more to
   me than to you, my lady, I would blanch and die, O
   Dulcinée.

2. Chanson épique (Epic song)
   Good Saint Michael, who gives me leisure to behold and
   listen to my lady, descend with Saint George upon the
   altar of the Madonna and with a ray from heaven bless
   this blade and its equal in purity, in piety, in modesty
   and chastity - my Lady!

3. Chanson à boire (Drinking song)
   Avaunt the bastard, illustrious Lady, who, to lower me
   in your eyes, says that love and good wine turn my heart
   to mourning. I drink to joy! Joy is the goal to which
   my steps are straight, when I am...when I am drunk!
   Ah, ah! ah! to joy! I drink to joy!

Nicolette   Ravel
   One of the greatest of modern composers has here produced a dainty bit of satire: Nicolette at eventide roams
   in the field picking flowers. She trips gaily along, when
   suddenly, she encounters a growling old wolf with evil-

gleaming eyes, who asks if she would go to her grand-
mother. Breathlessly, she flees, leaving behind her
mop-cap and clog shoes. Then appears a blue-eyed
gentle page, who shyly offers her his true love - nothing
more - but poor Nicolette wisely and reluctantly turns a-
way, sore at heart. Finally comes a grey-haired lord,
ugly, vile and corpulent, wheezing that he will offer her
all his gold...Swiftly she flies to his arms, our good
Nicolette, never again to return to the fields.

Pièce en forme de habanera (Vocalise)   Ravel
    Song without words.

Quatre Chants Populaires   Ravel
1. Chanson Espagnole (Spanish song)
    Good-bye, go my man, as they have taken you for the
    war. There is henceforth on this earth, alas, for me
    no myrth, no joy. Castille takes our boys, to triumph
    for it's cause. They leave as sweet as roses and come
    back as hard as thistles.

2. Chanson Française (French song)
    Jeanette, where shall we go and hide? Shall we have a
    good time? Down there, in the enclosed field, there is
    so much shade. The shepherd leaves his cloak and
    Jeanette can sit down. Jeanette has played so much that
    she forgot herself.

3. Chanson Italienne (Italian song)
    Leaning at my window, I hear the waves and think of my
    profound misery. I call my love, no one answers me.

4. Chanson Hébraique (Hebrew song)
    Mayerke, my son, dost thou know in front of whom thou
    standest? - In front of Him, the King of Kings and only
    King, my father. - Mayerke, my son, and what wilt thou
    ask Him for? - To have children, a long life and my
    bread, father mine. - Mayerke, my son, but tell me why
    children? - To the children one teaches the Thora, father
    mine. - Mayerke, my son, but tell me why long life? -
    He who lives, sings to the Glory of the Lord. - Mayerke,
    my son, you still want bread? - Take this bread, nourish
    yourself and bless it, father mine.

Sainte (The saint)   Ravel
    Concealed at the window of gilded sandelwood, where the
    Crucifix once stood, is the pale saint holding the old book
    showing the Magnificat which once was used for evensong.
    At the window an angel is touching the harp with her wings.

Musician of silence.

Shéhérezade   Ravel
1. Asie (Asia)
Asia, wonderful old country of the fairy-tales, where
imagination reigns like an empress. Its forest is full of
mystery. I would like to go away with the ship, rocking
in the harbour at evening, and which finally unfolds its
violet sails like a huge bird of night in a sky of gold. I
would like to go to the blossoming islands and listen to
the singing of the ocean in a bewitching rhythm. I would
like to see Damascus and the cities of Persia with their
graceful minarets. I would like to see beautiful turbans
of silk over black faces with shining teeth. I would like
to see dark eyes, passion-filled and pupils brilliant with
joy, in yellow skins like oranges. I would like to see
clothes of velvet and dresses with long fringes. I would
like to see the pipes in lips surrounded by white beards.
I would like to see ruthless merchants with squinting eyes
and cadis and viziers, who with a movement of their
fingers, grant either life or death. I would like to see
Persia, India and then China. The stout mandarins, under their umbrellas, and the princesses with delicate
hands, and the learned men, who are debating about poetry and beauty. I wish to linger at the enchanted palace,
and like a foreign traveler, contemplate at leisure, old
landscapes painted on materials framed with pinewood. I
want to see murderers, smiling as the executioner cuts
the neck of an innocent one with his large curved sword.
I wish to see poor people and queens, roses and blood, I
want to die of love, or of hate. And then, returning
home, relate my adventure to curious dreamers and, like
Sindbad, raise to my lips my old Arabian cup to inter-
rupt the tale with art.

2. La flûte enchantée (The enchanted flute)
Sweet is the shade, and my master sleeps, wearing a
silken cap, with his long yellow nose in his white beard.
But I, I am still awake and listen to a distant song of a
flute, which in turn pours out sadness or joy. My beloved is playing a languorous or frivolous tune, and when
I approach the window, it seems to me that each note of
the flute flies to my cheek, like a mysterious kiss.

3. L'Indifférent (The indifferent one)
Thy eyes are sweet like those of a maiden, young stranger,
and the fine curve of thy beautiful face, shaded by down,
is more seductive in its line. Thy lips are singing at my
door in an unknown and charming language, like music out

113

of tune. Enter! and may my wine strengthen thee. But
no, thou passest and from my threshold I see thee going
away, waving with a graceful gesture, and thy hips lightly bending, with thy step so feminine and weary.

Maria Wiegenlied (The Virgin's slumbersong)   Reger
The Virgin's slumbersong is a delicate little gem which
was inspired by the traditional German Christmas Song,
"Josef, lieber Josef mein." The rocking motion of the
mother's arms is beautifully expressed in the music.

RESPIGHI
Respighi was a student of Rimsky-Korsakov and Max
Bruch. His warmth and richly serene style made him
one of the most celebrated of the early 20th century Italian composers. His 52 songs are subtle, sensuous and
in the impressionistic style of composition.

Ballata (Ballad)   Respighi
Ottorino Respighi, the most prominent of the modern
Italian composers, knew - according to current opinion -
how to balance the classical elements of writing and certain reforming tendencies of his time. Here he has used
the lyrics of Boccacio for the setting of "Ballata," which
is from a group of "Five Songs in the Old Style."

"I do not know what I want - to live or to die! ... To
live is too despairing...I might lose you! To die...I
would not see your beautiful, lovely face..."

Bella porta di rubini (Beautiful lips like rubies)   Respighi
Beautiful lips like rubies, when you smile you reveal
shining pearls. You inspire love that inflames my spirit.
Beautiful little lips, as fresh as roses, do not speak nor
smile, so that we may feel the joy of our kisses.

Invito alla danza   Respighi
My lady, you are the ship of love that lightly skims the
sea of music; I am the robust sail. I bow to you and
invite you to dance.

Musica in horto (Music in the garden)   Respighi
A sound of clanging castanets breaks in rhythm the silence
of the rose garden, a flute trills liquid laments. The
melody, with silvery tinkling, is by turns sad and lively,
now light with restless trembling, now diffusing long, sad
shadows.
A joy of unexpressed songs appears to have arisen for

you from the closed gardens; and in the top of the rosebushes, the roses open like soft lips.

Nebbie (Mists)   Respighi
In the accompaniment of Nebbie, the shuddering chords
and harmonies describe the ghost-like mists and grieving
thoughts the words portray. The sleeping mists silently
ascend from the meadow, on high the crows caw and fly
over the grim moor. In the cold raw air, the desolate
trees offer their prayers with bare branches. How cold
I am. A dead moaning cry repeats to me, "Come to the
wide, dark valley, O sad, O unloved one, come."

Notte (Night)   Respighi
A shadow caresses an enchanted and perfumed garden.
All is quiet and the air shivers as the gloomy darkness
tells an ill-omened story to the chrysanthemums. Sweet
dew-drops fall upon closed petals which hide miseries,
lost happiness and muted dreams. Upon brief joys
crippled by disillusion the night cries her tears. Cries.

Pianto di Orfeo (Lament of Orpheus)   Respighi
Orpheus laments the death of his beloved wife, Eurydice.
He resolves that he no longer wishes to live without her
and bids farewell to the earth and the sun.

Stornellatrice   Respighi
Of what use is it to sing, "Birch flower, would that you
were the sun and I the star, going through the sky and
thinking of nothing," when the echo answers me, "Nothing?"
What is it worth to sing, "Flower of flowers, you are
my love of today and yesterday; you are my love that will
never die," when the echo answers me, "Die?"

RIMSKY-KORSAKOV
Rimsky-Korsakov was a member of the Russian "Big
Five." Being a naval engineer, he traveled widely through
the east and was deeply influenced by oriental color and
rhythm. His 80 songs, of a high level of excellence,
have a directness and spontaneity marked more by their
lyrical grace than their declamation. He was the teacher
of Stravinsky and Respighi, and the author of a treatise
on orchestration which has long been considered a classic. His accompaniments are picturesque and are highly
interesting because of their suggestion of orchestral color.

Aria of the Queen, from "Le Coq d'Or"   Rimsky-Korsakov
Tell me, oh all-seeing Sun, tell me of my native land.
Do the roses still bloom in splendor, do the dragonflies

115

still kiss the radiant leaves, does each maiden sing of ardent love near the rippling river? Is the stranger still welcomed? Does the unashamed maiden hasten to him with a tender promise on her lips?

Levko's serenade, from "Maynight"   Rimsky-Korsakov
Levko is serenading his beloved Galia, accompanying himself on the antique "bandura" (a stringed instrument of old Russia). He promises her that no one will see them. Should the night air be too cold for her, he will cover her with his jacket and will warm her with a kiss.

Little Snowflake's Arietta, from "The Snow Maiden"   Rimsky-Korsakov
How sad my heart! Lehl, whom I sent away, has gone to warmer lips. Dear Mother Spring, send me a spark of flame to melt this frozen heart.

Song of the Indian Guest, from "Sadko"   Rimsky-Korsakov
Sadko is a young minstrel-hero of medieval Novgorod. The Hindu Guest describes to Sadko the wonders, riches and magic of the distant East.

Song of the shepherd, Lehl, from "The Snow Maiden"   Rimsky-Korsakov
The snow-maiden, Snegourotchka, while gathering strawberries, suddenly disappears. Has the wolf eaten her? A passing stranger tells her playmates that she is hiding. But, alas, the little snow maiden is melting away in the sunshine.

Spring   Rimsky-Korsakov
The song of the lark is stronger and the blooms of the flowers are brighter. It is spring. The heart is lighter and the world sings with joy. Gone are the chains of sadness.

Sylvan rondelay, from "The Snow Maiden"   Rimsky-Korsakov
Hallo! I want to go to the woods and dance a rondelay led by Lehl. Let me go now and I'll return to sing you a gay song in the winter. Lehl will teach me to sing the song; it will not take long, my father!

The nightingale and the rose   Rimsky-Korsakov
A nightingale sings his song, day and night, for a rose he loves. So sings a lover for the one he adores, but the maiden does not know for whom he sings those longing, sad tunes at night-time.

The nymph   Rimsky-Korsakov
The nymph sings at night to the boatman and unties her
golden hair. Long after her song is over, when he is
far away, his wounded heart still hears the song of the
goddess.

The pine and the palm tree   Rimsky-Korsakov
On the bare Northern rock grows a lonely pine, snow
covered. She dreams of a palm tree languishing alone in
the sun.

Three Sacred Songs   Roman
1. I know that my redeemer liveth and that He shall stand at
   the latter day upon the earth. And though worms destroy
   this body, yet in my flesh shall I see God.

2. Whom have I in heaven but thee? And there is none upon
   earth that I desire besides thee. My flesh and my heart
   faileth, but God is the strength of my heart, and my por-
   tion forever.

3. But I will sing of Thy power, yea, I will sing aloud of
   Thy mercy in the morning, for Thou has been my defense
   and refuge in the day of my trouble. Unto Thee, O my
   strength, will I sing, for God is my defense, and the
   God of my mercy.

Star vicino (To be near)   Rosa
To be near the beloved one is the sweetest gift of love.
To be away from the beloved is love's saddest grief!

La cennamelle (Lullaby)   Rossellini
Alleluja! A child is born!

La danza (The dance)   Rossini
The day is fading and the stars are beginning to shine.
The hour of dancing and of love will come before the rising of the moon. Couples dance hither and thither,
bounding and leaping. Such pleasure leaves no time for
thoughts of woe.

Una voce poco fa (Recently I heard a voice), from "Il Barbieri
di Siviglia"   Rossini
Rosina has just received a note in which the mysterious
stranger, who has been serenading, attests his love for
her. His wooing has inspired her love, and gayly she
sings of her delight in the discovery. "Recently I heard a
voice. Oh, it has touched my very heart. I am sore
wounded...and Lindor 'twas who hurled the dart."

117

Amuri, amuri (Love, oh love)   Sadero
A tired laborer is returning home. He talks to his donkey. He sings of his love...And when the bells peal the "Ave Maria," he falls asleep...at last.

Fà la nana bambin (Sleep, baby)   Sadero
In the arms of your mother, sleep, sleep. Your father will come soon. If he does not come, I will weep, but you, not knowing, will sleep, sleep.

In mezo al mar (In the middle of the ocean)   Sadero
(A sea-chantey of Trieste - well known on the Adriatic.) "In the middle of the ocean is my lover, his heart being consumed by love as oil in the lamp - but I will not have him." Refrain: Cheer up, Jack, for I am the sailor's true love. "A tar's love is everchanging, if he were constant there would be no better lover." Refrain: Cheer up, Jack, for I am the sailor's true love.

Amour! viens aider ma faiblesse (O Love, come to aid my weakness), from "Samson et Dalila"   Saint-Saëns
O Love, come to aid my weakness. With your poisoned arrow I can reign supreme in Samson's heart. He will be mine and his fancy will never leave me. The strongest of men will tremble before me and be my humble slave.

Danse macabre (Dance of Death)   Saint-Saëns
Zig-a-zig-a-zig, death knocks on the tomb and plays a dance upon his violin at midnight. Skeletons rise through the misty shadows, and with arms and legs creaking dryly, dance to the whine of the violin. A lady, noble in life, dances with a pauper. Death removes class lines, the vassal and the monarch are equal behind the veil. The cock crows and the ghosts return to their tombs. Oh beautiful night for the poor world. Long live death and equality!

Mon coeur s'ouvre à ta voix (My heart opens to thy voice), from "Samson et Dalila"   Saint-Saëns
Like blossoms to the sun, my heart opens to the sound of thy voice. O love, speak to me once again; let all my tears be dried; let my heart now rejoice.

Printemps qui commence (Welcome joyous spring), from "Samson et Dalila"   Saint-Saëns
Welcome, joyous spring that brings love and flowers. Winter's gloom passes and gladness reigns. But I am sad, for my beauty does not bring me the one I wait for.

I weep while waiting in the soft night. If he comes, my despair will become gladness.

The nightingale and the rose (Song without words)   Saint-Saëns

Sin tu amor (Without your love)   Sandoval
Beloved, without your love what is the joy of living?
All of my life I will be at your side whispering, "I adore you."

Lungi dal caro bene (Far from my beloved)   Sarti
I languish in a sea of sorrow when I am far from my beloved. I feel my heart breaking. A deep slumber dims all light when she is away from my sight.

SCARLATTI (A.)
Scarlatti (A.) was one of the most versatile of the classic Italian opera composers. He wrote during the time when the virtuosi male-sopranos dominated the lyric stage. His arias are characterized by a serene and noble melodic line, with vital rhythms and classic form.

Chi vuole innamorarsi (He, who would turn lover)   Scarlatti
He, who would turn lover, should give it a second thought. Passion is a quivering flame, which carelessly lit can burn forever more. It is not a pleasant thing to have a wounded heart.

Già il sole dal Gange (Now the sun rises over the Ganges)
Scarlatti
Now the sun rises in splendor over the Ganges tenderly touching the dew of the morning. Its golden rays dispel the shadows of night.

Le violette (The violet)   Scarlatti
This song is sometimes known by the title, "Rugiadose odorose." Dew covered violets on the meadow, you peep through shadows and perfume the air from your gently moving stems. How you chide me for ambition.

O cessate di piagarmi (Do not hurt me)   Scarlatti
A mournful, sorrowful song pleading with cold, fateful and ungrateful eyes to hear one's plea.

Se Florindo è fedele (If Florindo is faithful)   Scarlatti
If Florindo is faithful, I'll surely fall in love. I can defend my heart from any living smiles, sighing, weeping and imploring, but if he should be faithful, I shall fall in love.

119

SCHUBERT

Schubert can be considered the father of the art song.
With him it became established and accepted as a form
of expression. Although over 100 performances of his
works were performed in Vienna during his lifetime, it
was not until after his death that his compositions were
widely performed. His first published song was dated
1819, only nine years before his death. He had a spirit
sensitive to poetic beauty, and expressed in his songs
deep personal emotion. His spontaneous melodies and
harmonies were a conjunct of his facile writing. In the
year of 1815 he is known to have composed 137 of his
over 600 songs.

Alinde   Schubert

She promised to meet me when the sun sets. I asked a
reaper if he had seen my beloved. He answered, "Wife
and children wait for me under the lindentree, I have no
time to look for other maidens." The moon arose and
she still did not arrive. I asked a fisherman for her.
He said, "I have to watch my nets and have no time to
look for the maiden." As the stars arose, I was still a-
lone and fearful because of her absence, and I called
into the night: "Alinde, Alinde!" The echo softly answered, "For searching so faithfully for her, you will
find your beloved." And suddenly she stood near me.

Am Grabe Anselmo's (At Anselmo's grave)   Schubert

That I have lost you, that you are no more, that my An-
selmo is resting in this grave, this is my sorrow. We
loved each other dearly and as long as I live, joy will
never return to my heart.

An den Mond (To the Moon)   Schubert

Pour, lovely Moon, pour down thy silver through this
green beech tree where fantastic shapes and ghostly
forms flee before me. Unveil thy face, that I might find
the place where my sweetheart rested and forgot the town.
Unveil thy face, that I might see the hedges under whose
cooling shadows she slept. Then, dear Moon, weep
through the veil of clouds - as weeps your lonely friend.

An die Leier (To the lyre)   Schubert

I would sing of Atreus' sons, of Cadmus would I sing -
but my strings are attuned only to love. I changed the
strings, fain would I change the lyre, so that its
mighty chords proclaim the glorious Hercules! But these
strings, too, speak of naught but love. So farewell, ye
heroes, for my lyre will ne'er waken to heroic song -

only to the strains of love.

An die Musik (To music)   Schubert
Thou noble art, in the grey hours of life, thou hast
lightened my heart with love and carried me to a better
world. Oft the sigh of a sacred chord from thy harp
has lifted my heart. Thou noble art, I give thee thanks.

An Silvia (To Sylvia)   Schubert
Who is Sylvia, that all the swains commend her? She is
holy and fair, wise and graceful. Is she as kind as she
is beautiful? Love goes to her eyes to help him of his
blindness, and being helped, remains there. Let us sing
and bring garlands to Sylvia, who excells all things that
live.

Auf dem See (On the lake)   Schubert
Blue sky, blue waves, vineyards around the lake, over
there the blue mountains shimmer with white caps. The
boat lifts and rocks us; mists rise and fall; sweet peace
lies over the bright world. Storm-tossed heart, look a-
bout you; you can find peace and happiness in the heavenly scene. The water mirrors steeples and hills, bushes
and the village; thus should you mirror in song the beauty
of the earth.

Auf dem Wasser zu singen (To be sung on the water)   Schubert
On the sparkling mirror of the water, a boat floats like
a swan. The rich tints of evening light the scene.
Gladness from heaven breaks o'er the soul in the red
glow of evening.

Auflösung (Dissolution)   Schubert
Hide yourself, Sun, that the fervor of delight may singe
my bones! Be silent, tones; beautiful Spring, fly away
and leave me alone! Sweet forces spring from my soul
- they embrace me, singing heavenly! Go under, World,
and disturb never the sweet ethereal choir!

Aus Heliopolis (From Heliopolis)   Schubert
Midst towering cliffs, dashing torrents, rushing winds,
the ruined castle stands. Here the poet breathes the
rarefied atmosphere; his soul drinks deep of passion and
when the mighty storm rages like clanging metal, his inspiration finds the right words.

Ave Maria   Schubert
Schubert composed settings of three songs from Walter
Scott's "Lady of the Lake," Ellen's "Ave Maria" being the

121

third.

"Mary, gentle Virgin, hear a maiden's prayer. Thou
guardest our slumber against the cruelties of man; Thou
makest of this rock-strewn wilderness a soft couch; Thy
smile spreads fragrance about us. By these the spirits
of evil are put to rout. Thy consoling presence fills us
with trust."

Dem Unendlichen (To the Eternal)   Schubert
How the heart is exalted when it lifts its thoughts to
Thee, Eternal One! How it sinks when it looks inward
to its misery, night and death! Infinite God, you lead
me from my night, Thou helper in grief and death. I
know that I am immortal through Thee. Tearfully en-
flamed, I know that no praise can be enough. Sway with
the tones of the harp, tree of life; sound with them,
crystal stream. Thunder, oh world, as a choir of trumpets; shine, oh sun, in all your glory. Yet, there cannot be enough praise. It is God, God, whom ye praise!

Der Einsame (The lonely one)   Schubert
When my little cricket chirps on my hearth at night, I
sit in contented peace, thinking of the past day. Chirp
on, happy cricket - you do not disturb me, for when
your song breaks the silence, I am not alone.

Der Erlkönig (The Erlking)   Schubert
A father rides through the night with his feverish son who
insists he sees and hears the Erlking (death) trying to
lure him away. The father tries to comfort him, but in
vain. Riding more swiftly, with fear and dread in his
heart, he reaches home. Clasped in his arms, the child
- is dead.

Der Hirt auf dem Felsen (The shepherd on the rock) Schubert
When I stand on the highest rock and look into the valley
and sing, an echo resounds from far below. The more
my voice sounds, the clearer it comes back to me. My
sweetheart lives so far away, my longing goes all the
way to her. I am consumed by deep sorrow, my joy is
gone through the woods and through the night drawing
longing hearts to heaven. Spring will come, the Spring
of my joy. Now I prepare to wander away.

Der Jüngling am Bache (The young man at the brook)
Schubert
At the brook's bank sat a young man weaving flowers in-
to a wreath, which the waves took from his hands; my

days pass restlessly, as the waves of the brook. Everyone is happy when spring arrives, but it causes deep
grief in my bosom. I look for one only - she is near
but so far away. Come, beloved, in the smallest hut is
enough space for a loving pair.

Der Jüngling an der Quelle (The youth at the spring) Schubert
Softly murmuring spring, you whispering trees - your
sounds awaken love from its slumber. From you I was
seeking comfort and forgetfulness of her disdain, and yet
the leaves and the brook sigh, "Louise!"

Der Kreuzzug (The Crusade)   Schubert
A monk, standing in his cell behind a trellis, dreams how
knights rode away on shining steeds, banners flying, voices
strong. They boarded a ship and it turned to sea as a
swan. "Like you, I am a pilgrim, though waiting in my
cell. This, too, is for the cross of strife, to win the
Promised Land."

Der Musensohn (The son of the Muses)   Schubert
Rambling through the fields and woods, piping my song,
here and there I go. To the lilt of the measure swaying
forth, my soul overflows. Wherever I find young folk,
I stir them up with my tune. Ye muses, winging my
steps - Oh, when shall I ever rest again on my beloved's
breast?

Der Schiffer (The boatman)   Schubert
In wind and storm I go forth on the river. My clothes
are drenched with the rain and I am scourged by the
waves with a mighty blow. The rapids roar as my boat
rushes on through reefs and whirlpools, but this is the
way I prefer it. A life of comfort is no life for me.
And even if the waves overwhelm me, I still like the
wild tempest that puts zest into life.

Der Tod und das Mädchen (Death and the maiden)   Schubert
The maiden sings, "Pass by! Go, wild skeleton! I am
still young, do not touch me." Death whispers, "I am a
friend and do not come to punish. You shall calmly
sleep in my arms."

Der Wanderer (The wanderer)   Schubert
I come from the mountains, my heart is heavy and I ask
myself, "where?" The sun here seems cold, the flowers
withered, and what they speak is empty sound - I am a
stranger on this foreign ground. Where are you, my

country, where my friends dwell - where they speak my language - where are you? I come from the mountains and I ask myself always, "where are you?" A whispering wind answers, "where you are not, there is happiness!"

Der Wanderer an den Mond (The wanderer to the moon)
Schubert
I, here on earth, thou, up in the sky, we both wander along sturdily. I am serious and sad and thou art mild and clear - what is the difference between us? I wander from land to land, unknown, without a home. But thou goest from East to West, passing all countries and art always at home. Ah, happy he who is always in his own home and country.

Der Zwerg (The dwarf) Schubert
Upon a placid sea a vessel floats, bearing a queen and with her, her dwarf. Sobbing, he winds about her throat a purple scarf. For a king she left him, now her death in payment he exacts. His farewell kisses sear as he tightens the scarf about her throat. What of his ship? No human tongue will tell!

Die Allmacht (The Omnipotence) Schubert
Great is Jehovah, the Lord, for heaven and earth testify to his great power. 'Tis heard in the fierce raging storm, in the torrents' loud thundering roar. 'Tis heard in the rustling of leaves in the forest, seen in the waving of golden fields, in loveliest flowers' gay array; 'tis seen in myriad stars that stud the heavens. Fierce it sounds in the thunder's loud roll, and flames in the lightning's 'quivering flash. Yet clearer still, thy throbbing heart to thee proclaims Jehovah's power. The Lord Almighty. Look thou, praying to Heaven, and hope for grace and for mercy. Great is Jehovah, the Lord!

Die Forelle (The trout) Schubert
This fable, in song-form, is the story of the fisherman who tried to catch a trout which, thanks to the clarity of the water, escaped his hook until he riled the stream. The agile, elegant swiftness of the trout is portrayed in the bubbling accompaniment.

Die junge Nonne (The young nun) Schubert
Loud is the tempest and wild the night. The thunder and lightning rock the convent walls. Rage, thou storm, as once it raged in my heart. But now all is calm for there is peace at last. My bridegroom comes, the heavenly

124

Saviour. Softly the Angelus tolls, calling like a voice from on high, to Heaven, my home. Alleluia.

Die Liebe hat gelogen (Love has deceived me)   Schubert
Love has deceived me and heavy lies my heart. Betrayed, alas, betrayed by all I held most dear.

Die Männer sind mechant (Men are wicked)   Schubert
Mother, I didn't believe you when you told me he was fickle, but he really is. You told me, "Men are wicked." When, at the edge of the village last night, I heard a murmur, "Good evening," and another, "Thank you." Mother, he was there with another. "Men are wicked." Oh mother, what torture!

Die Schöne Müllerin   (The Miller's lovely daughter)   Schubert
1. Das Wandern (Wandering)
Wandering is the joy of the miller, only a lazy miller would not think of wandering. From the water, the jumping stones, the wheels of the mill, we have learnt to wander.

2. Wohin? (Where-to?)
I heard the rustling of a brook, so fresh and clear, going down to the valley and I had to follow it. Is that my destination, little brook, tell me? Your rustling has intoxicated me. What can that be? Maybe the water-nymphs are singing and dancing down there. Wheels of mills are at every brook - let me follow along happily.

3. Halt (Stop)
I see a mill shining through the trees and hear the noise of the wheels. Welcome, sweet sound! The house looks cosy and the windows are bright. My dear little brook, was that what you meant?

4. Danksagung an den Bach (Thanks to the brook)
Was that what you meant, my rustling friend? To the miller's daughter I was sent. Have I understood it well? Did she send for me, or was it a spell? Whatever it may be, I have found fulfillment in my work and for my heart.

5. Am Feierabend (Restful evening)
Had I but a thousand arms, to turn the wheels and stones, that the pretty miller's daughter would notice my true feeling. Now, sitting at the round table in the cool and restful evening, the master says to us all: "I liked your work." And the dear girl wishes us, "Good-night."

6. Der Neugierige (The curious one)
   I cannot ask a flower, I cannot ask a star, they do not
   know the answer. I will ask my little brook if my heart
   lied to me. Oh, brook of my love, why are you silent?
   I only want to know one word - tell me, little brook,
   does she love me?

7. Ungeduld (Impatience)
   I want to carve the words in every tree, into all stones.
   I'll write on all paper and sow with seeds of cress,
   "Thine is my heart and will be thine eternally!"

8. Morgengruss (Good morning)
   Good morning, my beautiful miller's daughter. Why do
   you hide as if something were happening to you? If my
   greeting disturbs you, then I must leave again. Let me
   look from afar into your windows and see your blue eyes.
   The lark is warbling in the sky and sings of love and
   sorrow.

9. Des Müller's Blumen (The miller's flowers)
   At the brook there are many small flowers which look up
   with blue eyes. The brook is the miller's friend, and
   the eyes of my beloved are blue. That is why the blue
   flowers are mine. When she goes to sleep, then whisper
   to her in her dreams, "forget me not." And when she
   awakes, greet her lovingly, little blue flowers.

10. Tränenregen (Rain of tears)
    We sat together, happily, at the cool brook under alders,
    and looked down at the running water. The moon and the
    stars had come and we saw them mirroring in the water.
    The whole sky seemed to be in the brook and drew me
    towards its depth. Then my eyes overflowed and drops
    fell into the mirror. She said, "it's starting to rain -
    goodbye, I'm going home."

11. Mein (Mine)
    Little brook stop running, wheels do not turn and birds
    of the woods stop your melodies! Today only one rhyme
    sounds through the woods, "the beloved girl is mine!"
    Spring, are these all your flowers? Sun, do you have no
    stronger light? Then I am alone in all creation with my
    blessed words, "she is mine!"

12. Pause (Pause)
    I have hung my lute up on the wall with a green ribbon
    around it. I cannot sing any more, my heart is too full.
    Lute, rest on the wall and if a breeze goes over your

cords, then I am frightened and shudder. Is this the
sound of my previous longing or the prelude to new
songs?

13. Mit dem grünen Lautenbande (With the green ribbon of
the lute)
What a pity, the green ribbon is paling on the wall. "I
like the color green" - that is what my beloved said today. I will take it down and send it to her. I also like
the color green, because our love is ever-green.

14. Der Jäger (The hunter)
What is the hunter looking for at the mill's brook? Stay
in your own quarter, here is no game for you to hunt.
Here lives a tame doe, which belongs to me. If you
want to see the tender doe, then leave your guns and
dogs at home and cut your unkempt hair or you will
frighten the doe.

15. Eifersucht und Stolz (Jealousy and pride)
Where-to, so wild and quick, my dear brook. Are you
in anger following the insolent hunter? Turn back and
scold the miller's daughter first, for her light and fluttering mind. Did you see her last night, standing at the
gate, looking towards the road? When, from his catch,
the hunter returns home, no well-bred girl looks out the
window. Go, little brook, and tell her that.

16. Die liebe Farbe (The lovely color)
I will clothe myself in green, my sweetheart loves the
color green. I am searching for a wood of cypresses,
a heather of rosemary. My sweetheart loves the color
green.

17. Die böse Farbe (The vicious color)
I wish I could wander away into the wide world, if only
it were not so green in the woods and fields. Oh green,
you vicious color, why do you look at me with pride,
with boldness and malicious joy? I want to lie before
her door, in storm and rain and snow, and sing softly
day and night: "Good-bye." Take from your brow the
green ribbon, give me your hand and say, "Farewell."

18. Trockene Blumen (Dry flowers)
All the flowers she gave me should be laid with me into
my grave. Oh flowers, why are you withered and pale?
And why are you moist? When she wanders past the
mound and thinks in her heart, "he was true," then flowers, come out. May arrives - it is winter's end.

19. Der Müller und der Bach (The miller and the brook)
The miller: When a faithful heart is dying of love, the
lilies wither on all beds, the full moon hides behind
clouds, that one should not see its tears. And the angels cover their eyes and sob and sing a soul to rest.

The brook: But when love overcomes pain, then a little
star appears in the heaven. And three roses bloom,
half white and half red, and will never wither. And the
angels cut off their wings and go down to earth every
morning.

The miller: You mean so well, my dear little brook,
but do you know how love can hurt? Down below it is
cool and peaceful. Go on singing, little brook.

20. Des Baches Wiegenlied (The brook's cradle-song)
Good-night, good-night, close your eyes. Tired wanderer, you have come home. Here is fidelity, now lie
down with me until the sea drinks up all brooks.

Du bist die Ruh (You are the peace)   Schubert
You are the peace, the rest and longing, in thee I am
blest. When your eyes look into mine, my heart draws
near. Live forever in my heart.

Fischerweise (Fisherman's tune)   Schubert
A fisherman's life is a joyous one. He sets out in his
boat   before the lark has risen into the sky, and soon a
catch is in sight. He sings as he toils, but he who
would spread his net must have sharp eyes. Upon the
bridge a sly maiden is fishing. Pull in your line, that
fish cannot be fooled.

Florio   Schubert
Now, as the shadows lengthen and the breezes gently
blow, sighs emanate from my soul and hover over my beloved lyre. O Night, come closer to envelope me with
darkness. I seek rest which I yearn to find soon.

Frühlingsglaube (Faith in spring)   Schubert
Mild springbreezes blow again, carrying fresh fragrance
with them. Troubled heart, be hopeful, everything will
change. With every day passing, the world turns more
beautiful. The valleys are full of flowers; troubled
heart, forget thy grief! Everything will change.

Ganymed   Schubert
The mythical character of Ganymed, cup-bearer to the

Gods, who was carried to Olympus by Zeus disguised as an eagle, is used as a simile of the poet, borne heavenward in the ecstasy of inspiration. "To the stars, O mortal, take ye wings...The clouds float earthward, as though to meet my longing. Fold me, then, in thy embrace; then, I will rise to Thee, All-Loving Father!"

Geheimes (Secret)   Schubert
At the winking of my sweetheart's eye, everyone seems to wonder. I, the knowing one, understand the secret glances.

Gretchen am Spinnrade (Gretel at the spinning-wheel)   Schubert
My peace is gone, my heart is heavy, I shall never find peace again! When he is not with me, I feel as one in the tomb, the whole world is bitter to me. My poor head is mad, my pour soul is wounded. I look out of the window only in the hope of seeing him; only for him do I leave the house. His fine bearing, his noble figure, his smile, the power of his eyes, and the magic stream of his speech, the clasp of his hand, and ah, his kiss! My bosom swells for him, I long to seize him and hold him in my arms! Ah, could I but kiss him as I long to do, and perish kissing him! My peace is gone, my heart is heavy!

Gruppe aus dem Tartarus (Group from Tartarus)   Schubert
Hark, like murmuring of the wild ocean, waters are flowing through the hollow rocks and sobbing, and like a groan out of the depths sounds a heavy tortured, "Oh!" Pain distorts their faces; despair opens their jaws. With sunken eyes, their glances look toward Cocytus' bridge. And they ask each other timidly, "is this not yet the end?" Eternity swings over them its cycle and breaks the scythe of Saturn.

Heiden-Röslein (Wild-rose)   Schubert
A boy espied a rose, blooming in the heather. He drew near, to look upon it with pleasure. Said the lad: "I will break you, little rose!" Said the rose: "I will fight you with my thorns!" But nothing helped the little rose. Little rose in the heather.

Im Abendroth (In the glow of evening)   Schubert
How beautiful is Thy world, Father, when it golden shines, when Thy light paints the dust with glitter. Can I complain - can I doubt in Thee and me? No - within my breast I will cherish Your heaven. And my heart,

before it breaks, drinks the glow and the light.

Im Frühling (In spring) Schubert
I sit quietly by the side of the hill and look down into the green valley where once I was so happy and in love. Now all is changed and there remains only love's pain. Would that I were a bird in the tree there and could spend my days singing of the happiness that I once knew.

Lachen und Weinen (To laugh and to cry) Schubert
To laugh and to cry at all hours is based upon several reasons in matters of love. In the morning I laugh because I am happy, but why I cry in the evening, I do not know myself. I have to ask my heart.

Lied der Mignon (Mignon's song) Schubert
Only they, who have experienced longing, know what I suffer! Lonesome and unhappy, I look around - the one who loves me is so far away.

Lied eines Schiffers an die Dioskuren (Song of a boatman to the twin stars) Schubert
Oh, Castor and Pollux, twin stars shining upon my little boat, your mildness and watchfulness comfort me here upon the sea. Whoever is strong within himself and bravely faces the storm feels doubly courageous and blessed 'neath your rays.
When I return safely I shall hang upon the pillars of your temple this rudder that guides me through the waves.

Litanei (Litany) Schubert
All souls rest in peace after struggle and grief.

Minnelied (Lovesong) Schubert
The birdsong is sweeter when my youthful love wanders through the heather. Valley and meadow seem redder, the flower vases become greener when my beloved fills them with blooms of May. Sweet beloved, may you never leave me so that my heart, like this meadow, may bloom in joy.

Nachtstück (Night-piece) Schubert
Night falls, an old man, on his harp, intones a hymn of praise to its beauty and peace, its blessing of sleep. Soon it will be time for his last long sleep. One hears the wind calling, "Sleep well," and the grass whispering, "We shall cover thee." With these comforting assurances, he finds release in death.

Nacht und Träume (Night and dreams)   Schubert
Blissful night, ethereal dreams float in my breast like the
moon gliding through the heavens. And when awakening to
the morning light, those who have been blest by dreams,
call "return, oh, blissful night."

Rastlose Liebe (Restless love) Schubert
Through snow, wind and rain, ever onward, without rest.
The crown of life, joy without repose, is Love.

Romanze from "Rosamunde"   Schubert
The full moon is rising; my love, where are you? In vain
does May pour out her treasures, for you were all my spring.
Standing in the clear moonlight, she said, "In life apart, we
shall meet in death."

Schlaflied (Slumber-song)   Schubert
Forest and river are calling "You lovely little boy, come
stay with us!" The little boy follows and lies down in the
green grass. Nestling to his mother, the dreamgod puts
him to sleep.

Schwanengesang (Swan-Song)   Schubert
1. Liebesbotschaft (Love's message)
Rustling, silvery brook, are you hurrying to my beloved?
Dearest brook, be my messenger and bring her my greetings.
All the flowers of her garden refresh with your cool waters.
And when she, at your bank, dreams of me, then console the
sweet one, for her lover will soon return. When the sun
goes down, then cradle her to sleep and whisper to her
dreams of love.

2. Krieger's Ahnung (Warrior's foreboding)
Around me, in deep silence, my brother warriors are resting. My heart is heavy and full of longing. How often have
I dreamt sweet dreams, lying at her bosom, and how pleasant was the glow of her hearth. My love, may comfort not
leave you. There will be many battles, and soon I will rest
forever. Beloved, good-night.

3. Frühlingssehnsucht (Longing for spring)
Rustling breezes blowing mildly. I would like to follow
your airy path. Little brooks are flowing, like silver, down
to the valley and in the waves, the fields and the sky are
mirrored. Why does my longing draw me down? With restless, longing heart, filled with wishes, tears, lament and
pain, I am also conscious of a moving force. Who will, at
last, still my longing? Only you can release my feelings
of Spring.

4. Ständchen (Serenade)
   Softly and imploringly my songs go to you through the
   night. Beloved, come to me into the quiet woods. The
   tree-tops are whispering in the light of the moon. Do
   not be afraid of a betrayer, sweet one. Do you hear the
   nightingales? Oh, they beg with sweet sounds for me.
   They understand the pain of love. Let your heart be
   moved. Beloved, hear me, come and make me happy.

5. Aufenthalt (My abode)
   Rushing stream, rustling woods, rigid rocks: there is
   my abode. As one wave follows the other, my tears are
   flowing eternally. The tree-tops are moving like waves
   and my heart beats just as incessantly.

6. In der Ferne (From afar)
   Woe to the one who flees, goes out into the world, for-
   gets home, and hates his mather's house and leaves his
   friends. He will have no blessing on his path. Heart
   full of longing and eyes full of tears, thinking of home
   and sinking down hopelessly like the evening star.
   Breezes and waves, rays of the hurrying sun, which have
   broken this true heart, give greetings from the one who
   fled out into the wide world.

7. Abschied (Farewell)
   Good-bye, merry, happy town, good-bye. My horse is
   pawing; now receive my last greeting. You never saw me
   unhappy and it will not happen now, when I say farewell.
   Good-bye, ye trees and green gardens. Now I shall ride
   along the silver stream and loudly sing farewell. You
   never heard a sad song, I shall not give you one at parting.

8. Der Atlas (The Atlas)
   I, miserable Atlas, have to carry a whole world of grief.
   I have to bear intolerable things and my heart breaks
   within me. Proud heart, you wished for it. You wanted
   to be unendingly happy or unendingly miserable. And
   now you are miserable.

9. Ihr Bild (Her image)
   I stood in sombre dreams gazing at her image. And the
   beloved face came alive. Around her lips there was a
   sweet smile and her eyes glistened with tears of sorrow.
   Tears also started flowing down my cheeks and, oh, I
   cannot belive it, I have lost you.

10. Das Fischermädchen (The fisher-maiden)

Beautiful fisher-maiden, steer your boat to the land, come and sit with me, hand in hand. Lay your head at my breast and do not be afraid. You trust the wild sea daily. My heart is like the sea, with storm and low and high tide. And many a beautiful pearl lies in its depth.

11. Die Stadt (The town)
On the far horizon, the town with its towers appears like a hazy image in the twilight of evening. A moist wind ripples the grey waters and, with a sad rhythm, the boatman rows my boat. The sunbeams, reflecting from the waters, show me the place where I lost my love.

12. Am Meer (At the sea)
The sea was glistening, far away, in the last glow of the evening. We sat at the solitary fisherhouse, we sat there silently and alone. The mist came up, the waters rose; the seagull flew back and forth. Tears dropped from your loving eyes.
I saw them falling onto your hand and went down on my knees. From your white hand, I drank away the tears. Since that hour, my soul is perishing with longing. The unhappy woman has poisoned me with her tears.

13. Der Doppelgänger (The double)
The night is still, the streets are quiet. In this house once lived my sweetheart. She has left the town long ago, but the house is still on the same spot. A man is also standing there, staring upward and wringing his hands in pain; I shudder when I see his face, for the moon shows me my own self. You double, you pale fellow, why do you copy the suffering that tortured me at this same place, many a night in old times.

14. Die Taubenpost (The carrier-pigeon)
I have a carrier-pigeon which is devoted and faithful. It never misses its goal, nor passes it. I send it away a thousand times daily, to the house of my beloved. There it secretly looks into the window, watches her glance and step, and gives her my greetings and returns with hers. Day and night, the pigeon never tires. That is why I hold it fondly to my heart. Its name is: Yearning. Do you know the messenger of a faithful heart?

Schweizerlied (Swiss song)   Schubert
I sat on the hill, watching the birds; they were singing and hopping about and building their nests. I stood in the garden, watching the bees; they were humming and

buzzing and building their combs. I walked in the meadow, watching the butterflies; they were a joy to see, flitting from flower to flower. And then along came Hansel; I showed him what they all were doing, and we laughed and followed suit.

Stimme der Liebe (Love's voice)   Schubert
Love's angelic voice sings to me, "she will be yours!" My Selinde! Tears of longing change into tears of joy as I hear the heavenly voice, "she will be yours!"

Suleika
What means this stir? Does the East Wind bring me glad news? Its gentle whispers bring a thousand messages from my love, to comfort others in sorrow and in longing. There, where the high walls glow, shall I soon find my well-beloved.

Suleika's zweiter Gesang (Suleika's second song)   Schubert
Ah! how gladly, Western Wind, would I borrow thy dewladen wings! Thou canst take a message to him that I sorrow in his absence. Were I not to see him again, joy would leave my heart forever. Hasten, then, to my beloved. Tell him not, that I languish here, hide from him my pain and anguish. Tell him softly that his love doth hold me to life. Joy of love and life is mine when his loving arms enfold me.

Wanderers Nachtlied (Wanderer's night-song)   Schubert
Night descends in peace o'er the trees. Each trembling leaflet, e'en the breeze, hath slumber blest!...

Wiegenlied (Lullaby)   Schubert
Sleep, you sweet little boy, mother's hand cradles you. Sleep, mother protects you. Forest and river are calling, "You lovely little boy, come stay with us!" The little boy follows and lies down in the green grass. Nestling to his mother, the dreamgod puts him to sleep.

Winterreise (Winter-Journey)   Schubert
1. Gute Nacht (Good-night)
I came as a stranger and I leave as a stranger. May was kind to me - the maiden spoke of love. Now the whole world is sad and my path covered with snow. Why should I stay, as they drove me out? Love likes changes, my darling; good-night.

2. Die Wetterfahne (The weather-vane)
The wind is playing with the weather-vane on the house

134

of my beloved. The wind also plays inside with hearts,
like on the roof, but not so loud. They do not care
what pains I suffer, their child is a rich bride.

3. Gefrorne Tränen (Frozen tears)
   Frozen drops are falling down my cheeks, why did I not
   notice I was crying? Have my tears cooled so much that
   they turn into ice? They come from a glowing heart,
   which could melt the whole winter's ice.

4. Erstarrung (Numbness)
   In vain I search the snow for her footprints, where she
   once walked across green fields, on my arm. I will
   kiss the ground until my hot tears melt snow and ice,
   and I will see the earth.

5. Der Lindenbaum (The linden-tree)
   At the well, outside the gates, is a linden-tree. Under
   its shade I dreamt many sweet dreams and cut into its
   bark many a dear word. Wandering past, in the middle
   of the night, I heard its branches whispering, "come back
   to me, here you may find peace." The wind blew my hat
   away, but I did not turn back.

6. Wasserflut (Floods of water)
   Many a tear from my eyes fell into the snow. The cold
   flakes thirstily drank my burning woe. When the grass
   begins to grow, a warm breeze will be blowing. Then
   the ice will break and the soft snow melt. The little
   brook will flow through the town. If it feels the glow of
   my tears, it will pass the house of my beloved.

7. Auf dem Flusse (On the river)
   You clear and wild river, which rushed so gayly, how
   quiet you are now. And you give me no parting greeting.
   With a frozen crust you are covered, and you lie im-
   movable in the sand. With a sharp stone I engrave into
   the ice the name of my beloved and the hour and the day;
   the day of the first greeting and the day of my leaving.
   Around the name and dates is wound a broken ring. My
   heart, do you recognize your own resemblance in this
   stream? I wonder if, under its crust, it also tugs and
   swells.

8. Rückblick (Looking back)
   Though I am treading on ice and snow, my soles are
   burning. I do not want to take a breath until I have lost
   sight of the towers. I have stumbled on every stone in
   my hurry to leave town. How differently was I received

in this town of inconstancy. Larks and nightingales were singing, the linden-trees were in bloom, and the eyes of a maiden were glowing. If I think of that day, I will want to go back and stand quietly in front of her house.

9. Irrlicht (Will-o-the-wisp)
A will-o-the-wisp enticed me to go into the deepest rocky grounds. It does not worry me how to find the way out. I am accustomed to going astray, all paths have the same goal. I walk through the dry groves of the mountain stream. Every stream flows into the sea and every suffering will end in a grave.

10. Rast (Repose)
Now, that I lie down to rest, I feel how weary I am. My feet did not ask for rest, it was too cold for standing and my back felt no weight. The storm helped to push me on. In a small house with a charcoal burner, I found a shelter. But my limbs are not resting - their wounds are burning.

11. Frühlingstraum (Dream of spring)
I dreamt of colored flowers of spring. I dreamt of green fields and of singing birds. But when the cock crowed, I woke up and it was cold and dark. The crows were shrieking on the roof. Who made the leaves on the window-panes? I suppose you laugh at the dreamer who saw flowers in winter. I dreamt of love and loving, of a pretty maid, of embracing and kissing, of delight and happiness. But when the cock crowed, my heart woke up. Now I sit here, alone, and think of my dream. When will the leaves at the window be green? When will I hold my beloved in my arms?

12. Einsamkeit (Loneliness)
Like a dreary cloud, passing through fair skies, and a breeze going through the crowns of the firs - I go along with reluctant steps, passing happy and serene people, a- lone and without a greeting. Ah, if only the air were not so quiet, the world so full of light! When the storms raged, I was not so wretched.

13. Die Post (The stage-coach)
I can hear the post-horn sounding from the street. Why does my heart beat so strongly? The mail does not bring a letter; why are you distressed, my heart? Well, the coach comes from the town where I had a sweet love, my heart. Do you want to return and ask how things are going, my heart?

14. Der greise Kopf (The white head)
A frost has thrown a white glow over my hair. I thought
I was old and was very pleased. But soon it thawed a-
way; I still have black hair and have a horror of my
youth. How far away is the grave?

15. Die Krähe (The crow)
A crow came from the town with me, and flew around
my head until today. Crow, you strange bird, won't you
leave me? Do you think of grasping my body as your
prey? Well, this wandering will not last. Crow, show
me faithfulness to the end.

16. Letzte Hoffnung (Last hope)
Now and then, one sees colored leaves on the trees.
Often I stand thoughtfully in front of them. I glance at
one leaf, putting all my hopes on it. Ah, if the leaf
falls to the ground, my hope goes with it, and it makes
me cry.

17. Im Dorfe (In the village)
The dogs are barking, their chains are rattling; people
are sleeping, dreaming of things they do not have. Well,
they have enjoyed it and hope to continue their dreams.
Go on barking, you wakeful dogs, don't let me rest, I am
at the end of all my dreams.

18. Der stürmische Morgen (The stormy morning)
The storm has torn the grey cloak of the sky, the shreds
of clouds are fluttering around. Red, fiery flames are in
the midst of them. My heart sees its own likeness in
the skies. But it is only winter, cold and wild.

19. Täuschung (Delusion)
A light is dancing in front of me, and I follow it back and
forth. He, who is as wretched as I am, gladly follows it,
after ice and night, to a cheerful, warm house. Delusion
is for me a gain.

20. Der Wegweiser (The signpost)
Why do I avoid the roads where other people go? Why
look for hidden paths through snowy, rocky heights?
I have done no wrong and should not be fearful of men.
Signposts show the way to towns. I wander on, searching
for peace. One signpost is always before my eyes, point-
ing to the road from which no one returns.

21. Das Wirtshaus (The inn)
My path brought me to a cemetery. Here I stay, I said

to myself. Are all the chambers filled in this house?
I am weary and have a deadly wound. Oh, pitiless inn,
do you reject me? Well, then we must go on, faithful
staff.

22. Mut (Courage)
If the snow flies in my face, I shake it away. If my
heart talks to me, I cheerfully start singing. Let's go
happily through the world against wind and weather. If
there is no god on earth, we'll be gods ourselves.

23. Die Nebensonnen (The three suns) (meaning: Faith, Hope
and Charity)
I stared long at three suns in heaven. They stared back
at me as if they would not leave me. These three once
belonged to me, now the two best ones have gone down.
If only the third would follow. I should feel better in
the dark.

24. Der Leiermann (The organ-grinder)
At the outskirts of the village, an organ-grinder is standing. With icy fingers he grinds as fast as he can.
Barefoot on the ice, he staggers around, but his little
bowl is always empty. Nobody is listening and the dogs
growl at the old man. "Strange old man, shall I go with
you? Will you grind your organ to my songs?"

SCHUMANN
Schumann did not write for the vocal instrument until
1840. But during that year, the year of his marriage to
Clara Wieck, he found the composition of songs to be an
outlet for his own personal joy and wrote 138 of them,
the 26 songs of the cycle "Myrthen" in a single day! His
songs, in which the voice and piano parts are of equal
importance, are impetuous and have an harmonic origi-
nality and melodic intensity.

Aufträge (Messages)   Schumann
Little wave, little dove, and little crescent moon, carry
a message to my loved one - beg a kiss for me, which,
but for lack of time, I would beg for myself.

Dein Angesicht (Your image)   Schumann
In a dream I saw your dear angelic image. It was pale
and full of pain; only the lips were red. Soon Death will
kiss them to paleness and extinguish the heavenly light of
your dear eyes.

Der Nussbaum (The nut-tree)   Schumann

The soft rustling of the nut tree whispers of a bridegroom and of the coming year. The maiden, listening, falls smilingly asleep.

Der schwere Abend (The sombre evening)   Schumann
The dark and sombre clouds hung fearfully as we walked sadly in the garden. The night, hot and quiet, misty and without stars, was, as our love, good only for tears. When I bade you farewell, with sorrow in my heart, I wished death for you and me.

Dichterliebe (Love of a poet)   Schumann
1. Im wunderschönen Monat Mai (In the wonderful month of May)
In the wonderful month of May, with its bursting of buds and unfolding of love, I must confess the longing in my heart.

2. Aus meinen Thränen spriessen (My tears sprout flowers)
My tears sprout flowers, my sighs become a choir of nightingales. If you will love me, my little one, I'll give you all I have.

3. Die Rose, die Lilie, die Taube (The rose, the lily, the dove)
The rose, the lily, the dove, the sun, I loved them all - but no longer. You are the fine one, the pure one, the only one. You are all these to me.

4. Wenn ich in deine Augen seh (When I look into your eyes)
When I look in your eyes, fears leave my heart; when I kiss your red lips, I am whole and sound again. I was in heavenly peace when I rested on your breast, but when you said,"I love you," I wept bitterly.

5. Ich will meine Seele tauchen (My soul, I will sink)
I will steep my longing soul in the chalice of the lily until songs shall drift from its petals. The songs will thrill with the emotion of that blissful hour when our lips met.

6. Im Rhein, im heiligen Strome (On the Rhine, on that holy river)
On the waves of the holy river, the Rhine, the image of the great cathedral of Cologne is reflected. A picture in the cathedral has changed my life; on golden leather are painted flowers and angels around our holy Lady. Her eyes, lips and cheeks are like those of my beloved.

7. Ich grolle nicht (I chide thee not)
   I chide thee not, even though my heart will break for the
   love that is lost. I've known for a long time that no
   jewel's light can pierce the dull night of thy heart.

8. Und wüssten's die Blumen, die kleinen (If only the little
   flowers)
   If only the little flowers could know my sorrow, they
   would weep for my grief and woe. If I could tell my
   sorrow to the nightingales, they would sing a song of
   gladness to cheer my heart. The stars are too distant,
   for in seeing my pining, they would try to comfort me.
   All is in vain, only my beloved can heal my heart, which
   she has broken.

9. Das ist ein Flöten und Geigen (The flutes and fiddles are
   playing)
   The music is bright and the trumpets sound gaily for
   my loved one, who is dancing on her wedding day. The
   music is ringing and throbbing but the angels are sobbing
   for love that has passed away.

10. Hör' ich das Liedchen klingen (If I hear the little song)
    My heart recalls the old, familiar song which I fancy my
    love is singing. I go to the forest to hide my bitter
    grief. There my tears flow; I find solace and relief.

11. Ein Jüngling liebt ein Mädchen (A youth loved a maiden)
    A youth once loved a maiden who would marry another
    suitor. When this suitor married another girl, the maid
    then married the youth, but his fate was a sad one. It is
    the same old story, those, to whom it happens, can tell
    of a broken heart.

12. Am leuchtenden Sommermorgen (On a bright summer
    morning)
    I wandered in the garden, in the golden sunlight. The
    flowers gently nodding and swaying, gazed pityingly after
    me and whispered, "Do not blame our sister, suffering
    man."

13. Ich hab' im Traum geweinet (I wept in a dream)
    I dreamed I was weeping because you had died, and when
    I awoke, there were tears on my cheeks. Tears burst
    from my eyes as I dreamed you were leaving me, then
    I awoke and wept bitterly. I dreamed I was weeping and
    that your heart was still mine - now I awake and tears
    flow in an endless stream.

14. Allnächtlich im Traume seh ich dich (Every night I see you in a dream)
Every night I see you in my dreams. You, weeping sadly, look at me and give me a bouquet of cypress, the garland of death. I awake and you are gone.

15. Aus alten Märchen winkt es (From ancient fairy-tales it beckons)
A hand beckons me from distant fairyland, where bright flowers are blooming. Oh, if I could only journey there to gladden my heart and be free and happy.

16. Die alten bösen Lieder (The old wicked songs)
Get me a coffin, longer than the bridge across the Rhine, and twelve giants to sink it in the ocean; it is deserving of a large grave. Do you know why the coffin is so large and heavy? It holds all my love and my sorrow.

Die beiden Grenadiere (The two grenadiers)   Schumann
Two grenadiers were on their way back to France from imprisonment in Russia. When in Germany, they heard the sad news that their brave army had been defeated and their Emperor made prisoner. One of them, who had been travelling with unhealed wounds, said, "If I should die, take my body and bury it in the soil of my homeland. I shall, lying in my grave like a sentinel, hear the rumble of the cannon. And when I know that my Emperor is riding over my grave, I shall rise from my grave - and protect my Emperor."

Die Lotosblume (The lotus-flower)   Schumann
The lotus flower languishes under the sun's brightness and, with drooping head, awaits the night. The lover moon wakes her and she, blooming, weeping, exhaling, trembling with love and love's sorrow, unveils to him her face.

Die Sennin (The shepherdess)   Schumann
Lovely shepherdess, sing again your songs which penetrate even the breast of the mountains. Some day you will depart, through love or death, and the deserted mountains will sadly recall your songs.

Du bist wie eine Blume (Thou are like a flower)   Schumann
You are as lovely, pure and fair as a flower. When I gaze on you, sadness fills my heart. I would devotedly rest my hands on your head and pray that God will always keep you as lovely, pure and fair.

Frauenliebe und-Leben (Women's love and life)   Schumann
1. Seit ich ihn gesehen (Since first I saw him)
   Since first I saw him, I see only him; all else is colorless.

2. Er, der Herrlichste von allen (He, the noblest of all)
   He is the noblest of all, how gentle, how good! Just
   like a bright star in the blue depths, so is he, in my
   heaven, bright and splendid, sublime and distant.

3. Ich kann's nicht fassen (I cannot believe it)
   I cannot believe that he has chosen me from among all
   others!

4. Du Ring an meinem Finger (Thou Ring on my finger)
   You, ring on my finger, you have taught me how blest
   one may be by love!

5. Helft mir, ihr Schwestern (Help to adorn me, sisters)
   Help to adorn me, sisters! Make me lovely, to become
   a bride today!

6. Süsser Freund, du blickest (Dear one, thou lookest)
   Dear one, you look so wonderingly at me. Let me tell
   you my joyous secret!

7. An meinem Herzen (Here on my heart)
   Here on my heart, here on my breast, no joy on earth
   can be dearer or sweeter.

8. Nun hast du mir den ersten Schmerz getan (Now you have
   given me my first sorrow)
   Now you have given me my first sorrow, for you sleep
   in death. I have loved and have lived, now I live no
   more. I retreat into my innermost self - there I have
   you, my happiness, my world!

Frühlingsnacht (Spring night)   Schumann
   I hear the birds and the breezes wandering through woods,
   and that means that the springtime pleases. I would weep
   and then shout for joy for the spring has returned. All
   the wonders I have dreamed of are becoming awake in the
   moonlight. The moon, the stars are saying - and dream
   the glad refrain - Yes, even the nightingale is saying,
   "She is yours, all yours again."

Kommen und Scheiden (Coming and going)   Schumann
   When she arrived, her figure was lovely as the first
   green of the forest; and what she said, touched my heart
   as the first song of spring. And when she waved fare-

142

well, I felt the last dream of youth disappear.

Lied der Suleika (Song of Suleika)   Schumann
I sing, O Song, with profoundest rapture; I alone fill the
heart of my beloved. When thinking of me, his heart is
filled with bliss, without me his future will be lonely.
My heart is a mirror wherein his image shines, his endless faith, his love is a verse that reveals his noble
mind.

Lied eines Schmiedes (Song of the blacksmith)   Schumann
Little horse, I make you shoes. Be always happy and
devoted and come back again. Carry your master, always, on the right road. Carry him, with each step,
nearer to heaven.

Liederkreis (Song cycle)   Schumann
1. In der Fremde (Away from home)
From the homeland, behind the horizon, come clouds.
Father and mother are long dead and no one knows me
there. Soon will come the time when I will rest, too,
and above me will rustle the beautiful solitude of the
forest.

2. Intermezzo
Your image I carry in my heart. It gives me joy at all
times. My heart quietly sings a song which wings into
the air and hastens to you.

3. Waldesgespräch (The forest speaks)
The voices of the wood whisper the tale of the man who
met a beautiful maid in its depths one night. He attempted to woo her but upon becoming aware of her true
identity, the Lorelei, she turns on him and claims another victim.

4. Die Stille (The silence)
No one can guess or imagine why I am so happy. Only
one knows my secret. My desires and thoughts are more
peaceful than the stars or the snow. I wish I were a
bird and could soar far over the sea and upward until I
might be in Heaven.

5. Mondnacht (Moon-night)
It was as if the Heavens in silence kissed the earth,
which then must dream of Heaven. The bright stars
made shadows in the woodland; the breeze played upon
waves of wheat in the meadow. And then my soul in
wonder opened its wings and flew up yonder as if flying

143

home.

6. Schöne Fremde (Beautiful distant land)
The rustling treetops are shaking as if the old gods are making their rounds at the sunken walls. Behind the myrtles, the mysterious night speaks to me of wonderous things. The shiny stars speak to me of love and the distant land tells me of future great happiness.

7. Auf einer Burg (At the castle)
The old knight fell asleep at his watch in the castle. The rains fell and the forest roared. Ingrown are beard and hair and turned to stone his chest. For many hundred years he has sat in his quiet chamber.
Outside all is again quiet and peaceful. Everyone has gone to the valley where there is a wedding in the Rhine sunshine. The musicians are playing happily and the beautiful bride - she weeps.

8. In der Fremde (Away from home)
I hear the brooklets murmur and I do not know where I am. The nightingales are singing, here in the solitude, as if they want to tell me of the old happy days. It is as if I see the castle there, in the valley, and it is so far away! It is as if in the garden full of roses, my beloved waits for me - but she died long, long ago.

9. Wehmuth (Melancholy)
Sometimes I sing as if I were happy, but secretly, tears are flowing - they free the heart. Outside the nightingales sing their song of longing - all hearts are listening and rejoice. But no one feels the suffering and the grief in the song.

10. Zwielicht (Twilight)
Twilight spreads its wings, clouds float like heavy dreams. Do you have a friend here on earth? Do not be too confident, he may think of fights. What is bent today by tiredness, will be lifted up tomorrow. Many things get lost during the night. Watch out - and be cheerful.

11. Im Walde (In the forest)
A wedding came from the hill, the birds are singing. The horn sounds and many horsemen went for the hunt. Suddenly all was silent, the night was falling and from the mountains rustles the forest - and I am shaking.

Meine Rose (My rose)   Schumann
Lovely jewel of spring, rose of my joy, pale and drooping in the sun's hot rays, I bring thee cooling water
from the dark, deep well. Thou rose of my heart!
From the still rays of sorrow art thou pale and drooping. Would that I could pour out my soul to thee as I
pour on thee this cooling water. Could I but see thee
upright and blooming, lovely jewel of spring, rose of my
joy.

Mit Myrthen und Rosen (With myrtle and roses)   Schumann
Like a coffin, I would cover my book with myrtle, roses
and sweet-scented cypress. There I would lay my songs
to rest.

Requiem
He, who desired blissful union, has passed to the dwelling of the Lord where he will find rest from the pain and
deep longing of love. Starlight is falling into the grave
of the just, who, himself, will appear as a star in the
night when he sees God in Heaven. Holy souls, speak
for him; angels, sing joyful songs to festive chords!

Stille Tränen (Silent Tears)   Schumann
When you awake from sleep and wander through the meadows, the heavens are magnificently blue, but when you
sleep without grief, the heavens shed many tears. In
quiet night many a heart has wept and in the morning appeared to be always joyful.

Volksliedchen (Folk song)   Schumann
In the morning, walking in the garden in my green hat,
my first thought is, "What does my loved one do now?"
No single star in Heaven would I deny my friend. My
very heart I would proffer.

Wanderlied (Song of the wanderer)   Schumann
Come, let us drink the sparkling wine! Dear friends, we
must drink in farewell. An inner power leads me to
wander. The sun never stands still above, the tempest
storms fiercely across the land. I, too, must go through
forest and field.

Was will die einsame Träne   (Why the lonely tear)
Schumann
Why does the lonely tear? It is still there from old days
and veils my eyes. It had many companions, who left
together in the night, with my joy and suffering. Also
gone are the two blue stars who have given grief and

happiness to my heart. Love itself has gone - you old
and lonely tear, you may go too!

Widmung (Dedication)   Schumann
You are my soul, my heart, my joy and pain. You are
the world in which I live and my heaven. You are the
grave in which I cast all my past sorrows. You are my
peace and rest. Heaven guides me through you; your
glance has revealed me to myself. You are my good
spirit, my better self!

Lungi dal caro bene (Far from my loved one)   Secchi
Far from my beloved one I languish. I am in a sea of
sorrow. I feel my heart breaking. An extreme slumber
shuts out all light from me when she is away from my
sight. Ah!

Marinela   Serrano
Marinela, Marinela, with her song of sadness, consoles
herself to forget unhappy memories. She sings: "Be
certain before you give your love."

Svarta Rosor (Black roses)   Sibelius
O Night, set me free from the roses in my heart.
There is a thorn in the bud and a thorn on the leaf. The
petals of the roses have turned black from my aching and
grief.

Var det en dröm (Was it a dream)   Sibelius
Was it a dream that once I was your dearest love? The
memory of a wild rose you gave me, your tender glance,
your farewell tear. Was it a dream?

La Girometta   Sibella
Who made your shoes, Girometta? "They were made by
my love, who adores me." Who made your beautiful
stockings, Girometta? "They were made by my love,
who adores me!"

Sylvelin   Sinding
Sylvelin, God's blessing be on you day and night! As sunshine in the morning warms the fields, so have you
warmed my heart after a long time of grief and sadness.
Sylvelin, may God bless you forever!

Tonerna (The tones)   Sjöberg
Dark are the sorrows that come by night, and day brings
no release. Music alone brings balm to my troubled
heart.

L'heure silencieuse (The silent hour)   Staub
The silent hour is the secret and tranquil hour awaiting
the return of the herd, the hour when the good mother
is quietly sitting next to the cradle. This is the hour for
the tramp to beg for bread and for shelter. It is the
time when one sews one's trousseau, while dreaming of
living in the town. This is the moment of tender aban-
don, when Jean will join Ninon to pluck the petals of the
daisy. It is the troubled hour of evening when, without
seeing each other, Ninon, the tramp, and the poet cross
their paths.

Pietà, Signore   Stradella
Have pity, my beloved, and return to me. I cannot live
without you.

Pietà, Signore was written by Alessandro Stradella, an
important Italian composer of the seventeenth century, of
whom little is actually known, though he is the hero of
an extraordinarily melodramatic legend of jealous nobility,
paid assassins, and love pursued. Flotow made an opera
of this story. Stradella was also credited with being a
singer and poet, and a wonderful harpist.

STRAUSS
Strauss, although heralded as a composer in the larger
orchestral forms, was a significant composer of Lieder,
which are characterized by unconventional, flowing melodic lines and rich harmonies with a suggestion of orchestral color. Eight of his songs were composed with
orchestral accompaniment and the accompaniments of
eight other songs were transcribed by him. The subjects of his lyrics touch upon the ecstasies and sorrows
of the human soul. Opus 10, his first opus of Lieder,
contains some of his finest songs: "Zueignung," "Die
Nacht," and "Allerseelen."

Allerseelen (All-souls' day)   Strauss
Put the flowers on the table, bring the last glowing
asters, and let us talk of love as we did in May. Give
me your hand - I do not care who watches if you look at
me as you did in May. While every grave is fragrant
with flowers on All Souls' Day, let me hold you near me
as I did in May.

Befreit (Made free)   Strauss
You will not weep, but will smile gently as though you
were going on a journey; I shall return your smile, your
kiss. You founded these walls, I have made them your

147

whole world. Oh, Fate! You will grip my hands and leave your soul with me, leaving me behind with our children. You gave me all your life, I shall return it to you. Oh, Fate! It will be very soon, that much we know, we are made free from sorrow. I will give you back to the world and you will come to me only in dreams, to bless me and to weep with me. Oh, Fate!

Breit über mein Haupt dein schwarzes Haar (Spread your black hair over me)   Strauss
Spread your raven hair over me and turn your face to me; there flows to my soul the clear and bright light of your eyes. I spurn the sun's splendor and the brilliant wreath of stars. I only want the night of your locks and the lustre of your eyes.

Cäcilie (Cecily)   Strauss
If only you knew what it is to dream of kisses, of walking and resting with a beloved, of looking into each other's eyes, of caresses and chatter, you would soften your heart. If you knew the anguish of lonely nights, when the storms howl round and no one speaks a comforting word to a strife-weary heart, you would come to me. If you knew what life could be when it breathes the air of the gods, forgetting the world and soaring on wings of light to divine heights, you would be mine.

Die Nacht (The night)   Strauss
The night comes gliding from the forest, spreading darkness, bidding the flowers close, stealing the color from everything - even the silver from the stream. This is the time when sweethearts should be together lest the night take one of them.

Duet and trio, Act III, from "Der Rosenkavalier"   Strauss
Trio - The middle-aged princess learns of the attraction of her young lover, Octavian, to Sophia. She sadly gives her blessing.

Duet - Sophia and Octavian declare their love to each other.

Du meines Herzens Krönelein (Crown of my heart)   Strauss
Crown of my heart, you are pure gold, even sweeter with others beside you. They seek admiration; you are gentle and still. You charm everybody without seeking applause. Others strive to win love with worthless chatter, but you, using no skill to win men's love, are precious everywhere. Like a wild rose that never knows its loveliness, you rejoice the heart of every passer-by.

148

Freundliche Vision (Friendly vision)   Strauss
Not in slumber did the dream arise, but in broad day.
I saw it all - a meadow full of budding daisies, a little
cottage half-hidden in the foliage, and my dear one and I
walking hand in hand toward its abiding peace.

Hat gesagt - bleibt's nicht dabei (He promised but will not
keep it)   Strauss
My father asked me to rock the baby. He would give me
three eggs for supper. Of the three eggs he'll eat two
- and I won't be nursemaid for just one egg! My mother
asked me to tell on the girls and she would cook me
three squabs for supper. Of the three she'll eat two -
and I won't tattle for just one squab! My lover asked me
to think of him - he would give me three kisses after
supper. But three won't be all! What do I care for
squab! What do I care for an egg?

Heimkehr (Homeward)   Strauss
The breezes are softly sighing as the boat comes home
from sea. My heart turns to thee as the white dove is
flying to its nest. When the sun departs and night comes,
I turn, happy-hearted, to find rest with thee.

Heimliche Aufforderung (Secret invitation)   Strauss
Lift the goblet and pledge me and I will respond...After
feasting, hasten away to the garden where I'll meet thee,
and on thy bosom resting, adore thy beauty and drink thy
kisses. I'll twine around thy forehead roses white, oh
come, wond'rous, blissful night!

Ich liebe dich (I love you)   Strauss
Four noble horses draw our carriage; we live in a castle,
proudly content. Day dawns and lightning forks to show
us our domain. But should you ever be driven out alone,
in exile, I would share disgrace with you in mean streets,
hands bleeding, footsore, not a dog for a friend. When
your rich coffin stands before the altar, I will be laid beside you, but if you should die in poverty and loneliness,
I should draw my sword and follow you in death.

Ich trage meine Minne (I wear my love)   Strauss
I wear my love in silent joy. Since I found you, my days
are filled with gladness.

Liebeshymnus (Love-hymn)   Strauss
Hail to the day you were born! Hail to the day when I
first saw you! Beneath the splendor of your eyes I stand
in blissful dreams. Heaven seems to open and I see the

sun - I am longing. In your beautiful eyes I see my
image, how great my happiness! I pray, "Oh, stay with
me forever!"

Mein Auge (My image)   Strauss
Thou, my vision, dost penetrate my heart. Thou lightest
my weary, sorrow-aching soul and dost impart glory to
my life. Thy strength and purity hast made me whole.
I was blind to nature until Thou didst open my sight.
Through the splendor of Thy glorious mind I saw the
heavenly light of the world.

Meinem Kinde (To my child)   Strauss
As you sleep, I bend over your cot to bless you. Your
every breath is a silent prayer, an unspoken with that the
goddess of love will fly down and lay her lucky charm on
your white coverlet. As you sleep, I bend over your cot
to bless you.

Mit deinen blauen Augen (With your blue eyes)   Strauss
When you gaze at me, lovingly, with your blue eyes, I
cannot speak. It is as though a sea of blue flows over
my heart.

Morgen (Tomorrow)   Strauss
Tomorrow, the sun will shine again. Together, wrapped
in the heavy silence of our happiness, we will go hand in
hand toward that distant shore.

Nachtgang (At night)   Strauss
Arm in arm, we wandered through the quiet night. The
moon caressed your face with silvery light and you appeared as a Saint - holy and pure. I embraced and
kissed you. My soul wept.

Ruhe, meine Seele (Rest, my soul)   Strauss
Not a breath of wind is stirring, hill and dale are wrapt
in sleep. Rest thee, troubled spirit, thou hast suffered,
laboured, toiled. Rest thee, rest thee, O my spirit!
All thy sufferings will soon be o'er.

Schlechtes Wetter (Bad weather)   Struass
This is awful weather - it rains and storms and snows.
I sit by the window looking out into the darkness. A little
mother, with a little lantern, falters over the street.
She has bought meal and eggs and butter to make a little
cake for her little daughter who lies at home in the arm-
chair and blinks sleepily into the light.

Ständchen (Serenade)   Strauss
Open your door quietly. Come to me, in the garden,
where only the flowers and buds will know our joy. In
the morning, the rose will glisten from the joys of the
night !

Traum durch die Dämmerung (Dream in the twilight) Strauss
This song is one of those tranquilly beautiful expressions
that emanate only from the ideal collaboration of poet and
musician.

"Meadows vast in the gloaming; the sun has set, the
stars appear, and now I go to the most beautiful of wom-
en, far across the fields at twilight, deep in the jasmin
bower. Through the twilight, to the land of love; I go,
hastening not, but led, as by a soft velvet ribbon, through
the twilight to love's land in a tender blue light."

Wiegenlied (Cradle song)   Strauss
Dream, my sweet baby, of the heaven which brings the
flowers. The buds are glittering and listen to your
mother's song. Dream, bud of my care, of the day when
the flower opened, of the bright morning when your little
soul appeared in this world. Dream, flower of my love,
of the quiet, holy night, when his love's flower, turned
my world into heaven.

Wie sollten wir geheim sie halten? (Why should we keep it
secret)   Strauss
Why should we keep the happiness, which fills our hearts,
a secret. No, let everyone know the rapture which fills
our hearts.

Zueignung (Dedication) Strauss
You know, sweetheart, that I languish away from you,
that love brings heartache; for this, thanks. Once I was
free and drank wine to my heart's content and you blessed
the cup; for this, thanks. You expelled my evil spirits
till I became what I had never been before - holy, loving
you; for this, thanks.

Tilimbom   Strawinsky
"Tilimbom, Tilimbom," the goatshed is burning ! The
goat grazing in the pasture sees her home on fire and
calls for pails of water. The cat rings the fire bell,
"Tilimbom, Tilimbom." The hen brings a pail of water
and throws it on the fire. Mr. Rooster struts with his
pail singing, "Tilimbom, Tilimbom." See the crowd of
people coming - shouting and looking ! Come, good

people, help put the fire out! "Tilimbom, Tilimbom."
The goatshed is saved! Now the goat, the cat, the hen
and the rooster sit in a row and all sing, "Tilimbom,
Tilimbom."

Clair de lune (Moonlight)   Szulc
 Your soul is a fair garden, wherein gay revelers dance
 to the music of lutes. But beneath their fantastic
 masks, their smile is sad.

The Muezzin in Love   Szymanowski
1. O my beloved! Allah!
 O my beloved! Allah! Bismillah! I love you and my
 voice incessantly calls for you...Allah! Bismillah! I
 know that when the sun goes down, you wait for my soft
 call of Allah! Bismillah!

2. Olio! Olio! It is finished
 Olio! Olio! It is finished, it's ended forever, Olio! At
 this hour you felt the soothing kiss of the well. Your
 body is covered now with the burning sand of the desert.
 My heart is dying of longing and crying for your kisses.
 O my beloved! Olio! Olio!

TCHAIKOVSKY

 Tchaikovsky was a Russian who had deep ties with the
 German Romantic traditions. His music, which may be
 described as lush and overemotional, has an immediate
 appeal. His songs are characterized by strong accents,
 a sweep of melodic line and colorful harmonies.

Adieu, forêts (Good-bye, forests), from "Jeanne d'Arc"
Tchaikovsky
 This is the Lord's desire: I must follow His demand and
 obey Thy call, Holy Virgin. But why, my heart, art thou
 beating so fast? Why tremble? Terror fills my soul.
 Good-bye, forests, flowery fields, golden acres and
 peaceful valleys. Jeanne today bids you farewell forever.
 I shall be leaving and will never see you again. O sweet
 valley, where I have known so much joy, today I leave
 you. And you, my lambs on the green pastures, will be
 asking in vain for your shepherdess. On the fields of
 honor I have to guide the brave ones and gather the palms
 of bloody victory. I go where the voices are calling me.
 My heart is breaking, my soul suffers. Good-bye for
 eternity.

Lenski's Aria, from "Eugene Onegin"   Tchaikovsky

Before the duel, Lenski sings a farewell to his beloved Olga, as if he feels that the duel will be fatal to him.

Letter scene, from "Eugene Onegin" Tchaikovsky
Although not well, give me a pen and paper; I'll go to bed soon. Let me perish, but first, let me call for life's sweetness! I drink the magic potion of desire and dreams enfold me. I dream of my fatal temptor before me. How do I begin the letter? I write to you, what more is there to say? At first I wished to remain silent, but he shall know it all; it is not within my power to confine my ardent passion to my breast. She writes, "Why did you have to visit us; I should never have known you. If you had not come, I would have found a sweetheart and would have become a faithful wife and virtuous mother. But I can give my heart only to you. God has sent you to me; I saw you in a dream even before you came. When I saw you, my heart cried, 'Tis he!' Are you my guardian angel or temptor? I wait for a word from you which will revive my hopes."

Nur wer die Sehnsucht kennt (None but the lonely heart)
Tchaikovsky
Only they, who have experienced longing, know what I suffer! Lonesome and unhappy I look around - the one who loves me is so far away.

Toujours à toi (Always to thee) Tchaikovsky
Whether day dawns or night falls, I dream or see of life's pageant; wherever I go, the thoughts of my mind are of thee, always of thee. Griefs, that blighted my spirit, are gone, and love reigns eternally. Whether my days are joyous or sad, I have courage, hope and unselfish devotion. 'Till I die, in love's madness, I give my vow to thee. Only and ever to thee!

Adieu, Mignon! (Farewell, Mignon), from "Mignon" Thomas
Farewell, Mignon! Do not weep! The sufferings are soon forgotten. God will give you strength! My good wishes surround you! May you find home, family and happiness again! I depart with regret, and my hope is to see you once again! Farewell, Mignon! Do not weep!

Connais-tu le pays (Do you know the land), from "Mignon"
Thomas
Do you know the land where the roses and orange trees bloom, where the waves and the myrtle trees murmur beneath azure skies? Alas, I cannot go where I long to live and to die.

Duet: Légères hirondelles (Soaring swallows), from "Mignon" Thomas
Stolen, in her childhood by gypsies, from her ancestral home, Mignon has just received her freedom through the generosity of Wilhelm. The old minstrel, Lothario (her father in disguise), comes to bid her farewell, and, when Mignon asks him where he's going, he tells her that he is following the swallows southward.

Elle ne croyait pas (She did not believe), from "Mignon" Thomas
She did not believe that her innocent love one day might change to powerful ecstasy. To refreshen her burning heart, spring, cover her with dewdrops. In vain I search to discover her secret sufferings. My kind words frighten her soul and make her tears flow! My heart, warm her with thy sunshine!

Je suis Titania (I am Titania), from "Mignon" Thomas
Yes, this night I am the fairy Queen. This is my golden sceptre and these are my trophies. I am Titania, the blond daughter of the air. I wing over the world more lively than a bird and as fast as lightning. I fly my chariot at night and have legions of followers who sing of love and of pleasures. When morning comes, look for me amid the flowers, by the wood or on the Sea. I dance over the foaming wave and skip through the fog and mist. Behold, I am Titania.

Tu lo sai (Thou knowest) Torelli
Thou knowest how much I love thee, cruel one. I do not desire any other thing, only remember me. And then despise the faithless one.

'A vucchella (The discontented girl) Tosti
Your little mouth is like a flower sad. Give me a little kiss, my dear Cannetella.

Chanson de l'adieu (Song of farewell) Tosti
To depart is to die a bit...to die because of someone we love. We leave a part of ourselves at every hour and in every place...there is always sorrow, the last verse of a poem. To depart is to die a bit, and...though there is joy...until the last supreme farewell one's soul is torn at every parting.

Ideale (My ideal) Tosti
A dear one has changed everything in a lover's life to a happy dream. "Return, my sweet ideal, come back!

154

Come back!"

La serenata (The serenade)   Tosti
O serenade, fly to my loved one who lies half asleep.
The moon silently silhouettes the sails in the harbor,
the wave dreams on the shore, the wind caresses the
leaf, but my beloved refuses my kisses.

Marechiare   Tosti
When the moon rises over Marechiare, even the little
fish tremble with emotion. In Marechiare, there is a
balcony where the sea sings below. Your eyes shine
even brighter than stars. Come, awaken - I've brought
my guitar and will sing for you.

Voi dormite, signora (You sleep, my lady)   Tosti
Sleep my lady, under the branches that softly murmur a
song. While you sleep, the flowers caress you with
their perfume. Sleep, my lady, sleep on and on!

Novembre (November)   Tremisot
November returns! I sit alone and think with sadness of
our childhood and our triumphant dreams of love.

You in the heaven of my dreams   Vassilenko
Like a soft little cloud you pass in the heaven of my
dreams. I caress you in my thoughts. You are the sunshine in the gloom of darkness. You live in my endless
dreams and timidly blush in my ardent embrace. You
are the radiant sun in the darkness of my existence.

VERDI
Verdi, who achieved the greatest success of the Italian
operatic composers, wrote his first opera at the age of
25 and his last opera, the masterpiece "Falstaff," at the
age of 80. He had a strong sense of melody, drama and
a psychological sense of characterization. He was a contemporary of Wagner.

Ah, fors' è lui (Ah, perhaps it is he), from "La Traviata"
Verdi
This aria concludes the first act of La Traviata. Violetta,
young and beautiful, has just given a party at her house.
She is surrounded by a circle of gay and thoughtless be-
ings, like herself, who devote their lives to pleasure.
Among the throng who crowd to her shrine is Alfred Ger-
mont, who becomes seriously enamored of Violetta.
Touched by the sincerity of his passion, she yields to its
influence, a new and pure love springs up in her heart and

155

for the first time she becomes conscious of the misery
of her position and the hollowness of the pleasures in
which she has basked. She wonders if perhaps it would
not be sweet to give up her life of gaiety for the love of
Alfred. Then, suddenly breaking into her own mood of
tenderness and hope, she reverts to her habitual tenor
of thought, singing the brilliant and desperate aria,
Sempre Libera.

What folly! What can I hope for except love and sorrow?
No - pleasure, gaiety, shallow and empty joy of life are
my fate - I could not live another life. I can have no
peace or rest until I die!

Ave Maria, from "Otello" Verdi
Hail, Mary, full of grace. Oh pray for all who adore
on bended knee. Pray for the sinner, the innocent, the
oppressed, the wretched and the mighty. Pray for us in
the hour of death. Hail, Mary! Pray for us in the hour
of death. Amen.

Caro nome (Dear name), from "Rigoletto" Verdi
Gilda has fallen in love with the fickle Duke of Mantua,
whom she believes to be Walter Maldé, a poor student.
Dreaming of him, she sings, "Dearest name engraved upon my heart forever," one of the most exciting of coloratura arias, calling for extraordinary skill in the performer.

Celeste Aïda (Heavenly Aïda), from "Aïda" Verdi
If my dream would turn into reality and I would be the
chosen leader of a brave army...the victory mine! When
I return with laurel in my hair, I would tell you, beloved Aïda, "For you I fought, for you I won the battle!"
Heavenly Aïda, in my dreams you are the Queen, and your
throne stands near the sun!

Cortigiani, vil razza dannata (Courtiers! Vile detested race),
from "Rigoletto" Verdi
In Act II of "Rigoletto" (1851), the court jester, suspect-
ing that his daughter has been seduced by the Duke, con-
fronts the treacherous courtiers and demands entrance to
the royal chambers.

Vile and detested courtiers! You would do anything for
gold! For what price did you sell my jewel; my daughter
is a priceless treasure. Her surrender, though unarmed,
shall not be bloodless. Nothing is as fearful as when

God's children defend their honor. Tell me, Marullo,
gentle soul, where you have hidden her? Have mercy, I
beg. Return to me my daughter who is the whole world
to me.

Credo (Creed), from "Otello"   Verdi
   Boito's libretto is a condensed version of Shakespeare's play,
   suitable for musical setting, but remarkably true to the
   original in spirit. Iago, in malice, has just sent Cassio
   to Desdemona to get her help in winning Othello's pardon
   for his drunken brawling. Iago's soul is thus bared to
   himself.

   Cruel is the God that fashioned me in His own image, He
   who in wrath I worship. I must have sprung from a vile
   germ of nature, for I am not human. This is my creed.
   I believe as firmly as any woman who has knelt before
   an altar, but Fate drives me to think of every evil,
   whether I think it or do it. Honest man, your life is but
   a part you play wretchedly. Each word, tear-drop, kiss
   and prayer is as false as you are. Man is Fortune's
   fool; from the earliest breath his life is fashioned to
   feed the worm of death. After he dies, there is nothing,
   and Heaven is an ancient lie.

Di Provenza il mar (The sea and soil of Provence), from
"La Traviata"   Verdi
   In the second act of Traviata, Alfredo's father, the elder
   Germont, pleads with his son to leave the courtesan Vio-
   letta and return to his home in Provence.

Duet: Parigi o cara (Beloved Paris), from "La Traviata"
Verdi
   The dying Violetta hears the voice of her estranged lover,
   Alfredo, and, with a happy cry, she revives to join him
   in an ecstatic duet, in which they plan a new life together,
   far from the distracting gaieties of Paris. But the shock
   of reunion is too great for the frail Violetta, and she
   sinks rapidly and dies in the arms of her heart-broken
   lover.

Ella giammai m'amò (Her love was never mine), from "Don
Carlo"   Verdi
   Her love was never mine, yet I can still see her look of
   sadness when she came to greet me. My eyes are sleepless but slumber will come in the tomb. Oh, if the Gods
   would grant me the power to read the human heart. No,
   her heart is closed to me and was never mine.

Eri tu (Was it you), from "Un Ballo in Maschera"   Verdi
Verdi's opera, "The Masked Ball," was first presented in
Rome in 1859, with the definite intention of unmasking
certain political abuses.   Originally the composer had intended to make his scenes and characters Italian, to
leave no doubt as to his meaning, but under the existing
conditions this would have been too dangerous, so Verdi
wisely disguised his opera with a New England setting,
in Puritan times.   What would otherwise be an absurd
anachronism is thus at least partially justified.   However,
the scene of the opera is now frequently placed in Naples.

Renato is a loyal and trusted friend of the king and had
recently proved his loyalty again by saving the king's
life with great risk to himself.   Shortly after this, he
discovers that the king has requited his loyalty by in-
triguing to win the affections of his beautiful wife.   In the
aria "Eri tu" Renato expresses his bitter grief and disillusionment and vows he will have the king's life as the
price of his ungrateful betrayal.

Ford's monologue, from "Falstaff"   Verdi
The jealous Ford has been presented to Falstaff as Fontana, a man hopelessly in love with Mistress Ford.   He
gives the fat knight money, explaining that if only he will
"lay an amiable siege" to Alice, then, once she has fallen,
"Fontana's" turn will come for she will no longer be able
to use her virtue as a defense.   Falstaff accepts and
leaves Ford to give expresssion to his jealousy, cursing
marriage and all women.

"Cuckold!   The devil himself hath not such a name...I
will rather trust a Fleming with my butter, an Irishman
with my aqua-vitae bottle, than my wife with herself..."

Il lacerato spirito (This tortured soul), from "Simon Boccanegra" Verdi
The lament, sung by Fiesco twenty-five years before the
action of Act I, mourns the death of his daughter, Maria.
"This tortured soul of a father is doomed to the torment
of infamy and grief.   Pray, Maria, for me."

Io la vidi (I saw her), from "Don Carlos" Verdi
I have lost her!   Oh supreme power.   There is another
one, and he is my father.   She, whom I adore, has been
stolen, though promised to me in marriage.   How happy
were we in France at Fontainebleau, when, with hope,
we strolled together.   When I saw her smile, heaven
opened up for me.   Now forever, a father, a king, has

separated me from this heart. - Alas, I have lost her.

La donna è mobile (Woman is inconstant), from "Rigoletto"
Verdi
Woman changes like a feather in the wind! One never
knows what she thinks. Sometimes she is amiable,
graceful, in tears or smiling, but mostly a liar! But no
man can consider himself happy, who never experiences
her love!

Monologue from Act III of "Otello" Verdi
Otello denounces Desdemona and sends her rudely away,
astonished and grief-stricken at the strange, sudden
jealousy which has been aroused in him. He sings a
sorrowful soliloquy, declaring that nothing that fate might
have done to mar his fame or fortune would have been
so terrible a blow as this.

O don fatale (O fatal gift), from "Don Carlos" Verdi
O fatal gift, that in its fury heaven brings to me! All
hope is lost, my crime is past redemption, I curse my
fatal beauty! O my queen, I sacrifice thee to the folly
of my heart. Let me now hide, in a secluded convent,
from all the world my grief and shame. O heaven! and
Carlos? He dies tomorrow! But a day is still remain-
ing! Once more hope smiles upon me, to save his life I
will dare all danger!

O tu, Palermo (O you, my beloved Palermo), from "I Vespri
Siciliani" Verdi
The story of "I Vespri Siciliani" takes place during the
revolt of the Sicilian populace against the French and their
ruler, Charles of Anjou. The dramatic and tragic tale
unfolds against the grim background of the massacre
which occurred on the island. This aria is sung in Act II.

Oh, my beloved Palermo, my native country, once more
I greet thee after a long absence. With affection I greet
thy flower-covered soil and vow the allegiance of my
sword and heart.

Pace, pace, mio Dio (Peace, peace, my Lord), from "La
Forza del Destino" Verdi
In this aria, taken from the fourth act, Leonora, torn be-
tween her love for her father and her love for Alvaro,
who was the innocent cause of her father's death, implores
Heaven to let her die.

Per me giunto (United with you), from "Don Carlos" Verdi
Rodrigo visits Carlo in prison, telling him that he has
sacrificed himself in coming to save him. "You will
reign over Spain and Flanders, bringing them to a new
golden age. Gladly I die that our cause may be de-
fended."

Pietà, rispetto, amore (Compassion, honor, love), from
"Macbeth" Verdi
As Shakespeare's tragedy and Verdi's opera draw to a
close, Macbeth's world is crumbling about him. He is
alone in a hall of the palace, and as he prepares to
meet his enemies in the final battle, his only comfort is
the witches' prophecy that no man born of woman shall
harm him:

"My way of life has withered as the yellow leaf, and that
which should accompany old age, compassion, honor, love
and friends, I cannot have."

Questa o quella (This one or that one), from "Rigoletto"
Verdi
With charming impudence the Duke sings this gay song of
his numerous loves. "This one or that one - it makes
no difference. If with one maid I am happy today, tomorrow, another I'll find."

Re dell' abisso (King of Hades), from "Un Ballo in Maschera"
Verdi
In her den, Ulrica, the soothsayer, looks into the future.
She addresses herself to the King of Hades and proudly
boasts that there is nothing which he can keep hidden
from her.

Richard's barcarolle from "Un Ballo in Maschera" Verdi
King Richard, disguised as a sailor, and his friends go
to visit an accused witch. He is amused at the old woman's magic and sings a taunting barcarolle, asking her
questions about his supposed future, with bantering good
humor.

Ritorna vincitor (Return victorious), from "Aïda" Verdi
Aïda, secretly in love with the hero, Rhadames, wishes
to speed him on his way against the foe. Yet, even as
she sings "Return victorious," she realizes that if he
does so, it will mean the destruction of her own land
and the defeat of her father. Her soul is tormented and
her heart torn between love for Rhadames and for her
home.

Stride la vampa (Fiercely the flames burn), from 'Il Trovatore" Verdi
The flames burn fiercely and the wild crowd roars for vengeance. The flames and swirling smoke dash heavenward as the barefoot and helpless victim is led to death.

Trio: Perdon, perdon, Amelia (Forgive, forgive, Amelia), from "Simon Boccanegra" Verdi
When Gabriele, blind with jealousy - for he blieves Amelia in love with Simon - attempts to kill his suspected rival, Amelia rushes in and reveals the true relationship. The Doge, Simon is her father. From Amelia, Gabriele begs forgiveness and from the Doge, death, because of his unworthiness, while Amelia calls on Heaven to protect him who is guilty only because of his great love. Simon questions his own course of action and accepts Gabriele as his friend.

Trio: Qual voluttà trascorrere (What unending joy), from 'I Lombardi" Verdi
Giselda and Oronte have fled from the Crusaders to the mountains where they are befriended by Pagano, the hermit. Pagano asks the fugitives to turn their fainting hearts to God so that they may meet in Heaven, and, as Oronte, mortally wounded, promises to wait in Heaven for his love, Giselda prays that the pitying angels will join their spirits once again.

Mokocê-cê-makâ (Native lullaby) Villa-Lobos
The native mother, after affectionately rocking her small son to sleep, shows her happiness at seeing his restful slumber.

Nhapopê Villa-Lobos
There is an old song that Nhapopê, the goddess, on white moonlit nights, comes down to the earth and seeks comfort in a human heart. "You are Nhapopê, I love you and you can trust me."

Redondhilha Villa-Lobos
Vengeful life calls me and kisses me, then slips through my fingers and deceives me. I love, I suffer, I flee and return, I cry and rebel. I think, I walk, I drink and I forget...

Xangô Villa-Lobos
Negro song of black magic.

Un certo non so che (A certain thing)   Vivaldi
A certain thing reaches for and passes my heart, and
yet it is not pain.   Could this be love?   With its vora-
cious ardour it already incautiously puts down its foot.

WAGNER
Wagner is primarily known for his music dramas in
which there is the highest integration of all of the arts.
He placed great importance on the text of his dramas
and was always mindful of the close relationship between
the natural accents of the language and those of the music.   The search for this integration may be one of the
reasons he wrote his own libretti.   His music has been
described as having "heroic strength, loveliness, nobility
and epic grandeur."

Allmächt'ge Jungfrau (Almighty Virgin), from "Tannhäuser"
Wagner
Almighty Virgin, hear my plea!   To thee I call!   Let
me perish in dust before thee!   Let me, pure and angel-
like, enter into thy blessed kingdom!   If ever my heart
turned away from thee, if ever a sinful desire, a worldly longing sprang up in me, I struggled with a thousand
pangs to kill it in my heart.   In thy mercy accept me,
that I may approach thee as a worthy maiden and implore
thy mercy for his offense.

Am stillen Herd (On the quiet hearth), from "Die Meister-
singer"   Wagner
On the quiet hearth in winter, when castle and court were
snowed in, I often read in an old book by Walter von der
Vogelweide - he was my master.   When the fields
thawed and summer returned, I remembered what the old
book taught me in winter and sang loudly out into the
woods.   And that is how I learned to sing.   What the
winter night, the beauty of the woods and my book taught
me, gave me food for thought.   Through song I wish to
win the highest prize with my own word and my own melody.   It shall be a master-song.

Dich, teure Halle (Dear, beloved hall), from "Tannhäuser)
Wagner
Dear beloved hall, I greet thee!   Sound his songs and
roused me from gloomy dream.   When he departed from
thee, how desolate didst thou seem to me!   Peace fled
from me, joy departed from thee!   How my bosom now
swells, so now thou seemst proud and lofty; he who brings
new life to me and thee, no longer tarries far away!

Die Frist ist um (The term is past), from "Der Fliegende
Holländer"   Wagner
   The Flying Dutchman, in a maritime legend of the wandering Jew, has been condemned to eternally sail the
   seas until he finds a faithful wife. He is allowed, under
   the curse, to land once in every seven years, to search
   for a spouse who will absolve him from his tragic fate.
   In this aria, he laments his tireless journey and tells
   how he has longed for his doom, courting death by the
   sword of the pirate and by other dangers. "I look for
   the kind angel who will free me - but there is no hope.
   Oh, Judgement Day, when the dead arise, then shall I
   find destruction, then shall I attain the eternal end of all."

Du bist der Lenz (Thou art the spring), from "Die Walküre"
Wagner
   Thou art the Spring for which I longed during frosty Winter's term. My heart did greet thee when thy glance
   first fell on me. I recognized thee plainly and clearly;
   as soon as my eyes saw thee, thou wert mine own.

Einsam in trüben Tagen (Lonely in days of sorrow), from
"Lohengrin" Wagner
   Lonely, in days of sorrow I prayed to God. From my
   plaint rose a grief-filled sound that swelled far into the
   sky. My eyes closed, I sank in sweet slumber. In
   bright shining armor a knight drew near, one I had never
   seen before; a golden horn at his hip, leaning on his
   sword - he advanced from the sky to me and gave me
   comfort; he shall be my protector! Hear what I offer as
   a pledge to this emissary of God: in my father's lands
   he will bear the crown and, if he wish, I shall be his
   wife.

Euch Lüften, die mein Klagen (Ye breezes who have heard
my plaint), from "Lohengrin" Wagner
   Ye breezes who have often heard my plaint, I must thank-
   fully tell how my happiness was revealed! By ye he was
   borne, ye smiled upon the journey; on the wild waves ye
   faithfully guarded him. To dry my tears I have often
   troubled you; coolness now grant to my cheek which is
   aglow with love.

Morgenlicht leuchtend (The morning shone), from "Die Meis-
tersinger" Wagner
   The morning shone with rosy light, the air was full with
   scent of flowers. A garden invited me, where, under a
   wondrous fruit tree, I saw in blissful love-dream the
   most beautiful woman: Eva - in paradise. In the eve-

ning twilight   I came to a fountain, which attracted me.
There, under a laurel-tree, a poetic vision greeted me,
the fairest woman: Parnassus, the Muse.   Sweetest day,
to which I awoke from a poet's dream, I had dreamt of
paradise in heavenly and new beauty.   The fairest image,
my holy muse, to whom I am dedicated, shall be wooed
by me, through my victorious song: Parnassus and
Paradise.

O du mein holder Abendstern (O you my friendly evening
star), from "Tannhäuser"   Wagner
In the last act of Tannhäuser, the minstrel-knight, Wolf-
ram, sings his Song to the Evening Star, committing to
its protection his beloved Elizabeth, who is dying of love
for his friend, Tannhäuser. - "Shine on, oh star, bright
star of eve.   Sing to her beyond the sky that love, true
love, will never die.

Wesendonck Lieder (Wesendonck Songs)   Wagner
1. Der Engel (The angel)
When I was a child I heard stories of angels who ex-
changed Heaven's bliss for earth's sunlight.   Wherever a
prayer is offered, begging for release, the angel sweeps
down and carries the pained one to heaven.   The angel
is now bearing my spirit upward away from all pain.

2. Stehe still! (Stand still)
Brilliant planets of the wide universe, oh creation, cease
your growing.   Leave me alone that I may measure all
bliss.   When we gaze into each other's eyes, may we
reach the fulfillment of our hopes.

3. Im Treibhaus (In the greenhouse)
High arches of green, bowing in sorrow, you spread your
branches in horror of dreary emptiness.   Poor trees, we
share the same fate, for our home is not here.   Heavy
drops of dew are gathering on your leaves.

4. Schmerzen (Pains)
Sun, you weep until your eyes are red in the mirror of
the sea, but you arise victorious in the morning.   Why
should I despair to find my heart so heavy, if the sun itself must descend.   For if death, only, can bring life,
and only pain bring forth joy, I thank you that I have been
given such pain!

5. Träume (Dreams)

My spirit is held fast in bondage by dreams of mystical enchantment. These dreams, which do not sink into twilight, grow in greater wonder ever hour and, with heavenly magic, draw the soul to higher ecstasy. They are visions that with radiant beams paint a fair, eternal image upon the heart. Visions more lasting than the crimson roses which the sun calls from darkness at dawn; roses which glow an hour and then fall to dust.

Winterstürme wichen dem Wonnemond (Winterstorms gave way to spring), from "Die Walküre" Wagner
Winterstorms gave way to spring which brought sweet breezes that work wonders. With delicate weapons Spring has conquered the world - winter and storm had to vanish. To his sister, the brother was drawn, love enticed by Spring. The bridal sister is freed by her brother. Exulting the young couple greet each other, reunited are love and Spring.

Durch die Wälder, durch die Auen (Through the forests, through the meadows), from "Der Freischütz" Weber
No longer can I bear the suffering, the fear, which banish all hope! What is the fault I am punished for? Through the forests, through the meadows I strayed lighthearted. Everything I wanted was my rifle's certain prey. When at evening I returned, Agatha greeted me with love in her eyes. Has heaven forsaken me? Am I doomed to be destroyed? - Right now, I'm sure, she waits at the open window for my step, hoping, that her Max will bring good news. But what evil powers take hold of me? No light will shine through these nights? Fate dictates. Where is God?

Leise, leise, fromme Weise (Gentle melody, soar to the stars), from "Der Freischütz" Weber
The story of the opera is founded on an old tradition among huntsmen in Germany that whoever shall sell his soul to Zamiel, the Demon Hunter, will receive seven magic bullets which always hit the mark. Unknown to Agatha, Max is about to make this perilous compact, and, while anxiously awaiting his coming, she opens the window and exclaims at the wonder of the beautiful starlight night and then sings her expressive prayer.

"How can I fall asleep, before I have seen him? Yes, love goes always with sorrow, hand in hand. The moon lights his path - what a beautiful night! Gentle melody, soar to the stars and take my prayers to heaven! How bright the stars are shining. Only in the distance, over

the mountains, are dark clouds. Lord, I pray, send
Thy angels to protect us! All is quiet and restful!
Where is my beloved? Now I hear steps, from the pines
someone approaches! It is he! He seems not to see
me. If I'm not mistaken, I see flowers around his hat!
He certainly won a prize at the shooting-range! Oh,
hope! My heart beats loud and waits for him! Could I
dare to hope? Yes, good luck smiles at the beloved
friend! Heaven, be praised and accept my grateful tears
for the new hope!"

WOLF

Wolf was a great admirer of Wagner and was deeply influenced by him. Although a composer of two unsuccess-
ful operas, each of his songs is a diminutive music
drama with vivid characterization. His melodic line is a
faithful portrayal of the words, their accents and stress.
In speaking of his songs, he stated that, "Poetry is the
true source of my music." After having been moved by
a poem he would write a song in immediate inspiration,
seldom rescoring it. He composed songs by few poets,
for he felt that by setting many songs of the same poet,
he could better know the inner meanings of their lyrics.
The accompaniments are intricate and at times may over-
shadow the vocal line. He was cognizant of orchestral
color, having orchestrated 20 of his 275 songs.

Abschied (Goodby!)   Wolf
Quite unannounced, a gentleman called on me, "I have the
great honor, Sir, to be your critic." So he took the candle and gazed at my shadow on the wall. "Now, young
man, observe how dreadful your nose is. That is truly a
protuberance." "What? Good heavens, 'tis true! I never
knew that such a nose grew on my face." The man
talked on and on, but I understood nothing more. Finally
he rose. At the top of the stairs I gave him a nice little
kick in the seat of his pants! Heavens! I have never
seen a man go down the stairs so quickly!

Ach, des Knaben Augen (Ah, how fair the Infant eyes)   Wolf
The eyes of the blessed Child are so clear and beautiful;
their beauty captivates my heart. When He gazes into
His mother's eyes, does He see His likeness there?

Alle gingen, Herz, zur Ruh (Everyone is sleeping)   Wolf
Everyone is sleeping, but you, my heart! Hopeless grief
kills your sleep, and your thoughts, in mute grief, wander towards your love.

166

Anakreon's Grab (Anacreon's grave)   Wolf
Where roses bloom, vines entwine, where turtle-doves
coo and crickets chirp - 'tis here Anacreon sleeps.
Autumn, summer and spring made glad the heart of the
poet. Now beneath this mound he is sheltered from
Winter forever.

An eine Aeolsharfe. (The aeolian harp)   Wolf
The wind which resounds through my aeolian harp comes
from afar and brings the yearning of my beloved one. In
sweet alarm I feel my own longing - stirred by the delicate breeze which sings in the aeolian harp; the full-
blown rose scatters its petals at my feet.

Auch kleine Dinge (E'en little things)   Wolf
E'en little things may give us pleasure...Above all gems,
the little pearl we treasure - the fairest of all flowers,
the rosebud sweet.

Auf ein altes Bild (Looking at an old painting)   Wolf
Here, where the meadows are green in summer, where
the cooling waters flow, look how the child, free of sins,
is playing on the Virgin's knee! And there, in the forest, already grows the cross!

Auf eine Christblume (To a Christmas-flower)   Wolf
Daughter of the woods, so like a lily, after a long search
I have found you in this churchyard. Who has tended
you, whose grave do you adorn? You have been nourished by the heavenly coldness and the sweet balsam air.
You are fragrant and dressed in the bridal gown of the
Blessed Virgin. In token of the Holy Passion of our Lord,
five purple drops adorn your simple robe. But childlike
you adorn your white dress at Christmastime with green.
The elves stand timidly still and curious before your
mystical glory and quietly hasten away.

Auf einer Wanderung (Wandering)   Wolf
To a friendly town I come at eve, from an open window
I hear a sweet voice singing. Long did I linger - then
somehow changed, I went my way. Oh Muse, an ecstasy
of love invaded my heart.

Bedeckt mich mit Blumen (Cover me with flowers)   Wolf
Cover me with flowers - I die of love. So that the air
with its soft winds shall not bear away the sweet perfume
- cover me! It is all the same - the breath of love or
the scent of flowers. Prepare here my grave of jasmine
and white lilies - I die. And if you ask me, "of what?"

167

I say, "of love's sweet torments. Of love."

Begegnung (The meeting)   Wolf
What a storm that was last night! How it swept everything away. A shy and pretty girl comes down the street
this morning and a handsome boy approaches her. Happily and confusedly they glance at each other dreaming of
all those kisses and what happened between them during
the storm.

Bei einer Trauung (At a wedding)   Wolf
A wedding before a select and aristocratic congregation,
the bride weeping bitterly, the bridegroom with a dreadful expression. Alas, there is no love between them.

Bescheidene Liebe (Unpretentious love)   Wolf
I am not like other maidens, who, when they love, keep
sighing. I am not tongue-tied; and love in my own fash-
ion. I let the whole world see that I am in love. I am
not like other maidens - I am happy because I am not
seeking ring nor protection.

Das verlassene Mägdlein. (The deserted maiden)   Wolf
I awake, weary and tired, and go about my morning
tasks. Suddenly I realize that again, last night, I
dreamed of you, faithless one! Tears stream down my
cheeks and I know that life is empty without you.

Denk es, o Seele (Remember, my soul)   Wolf
A little pinetree grows somewhere in the forest, a rose-
bush somewhere in the garden. They are already chosen,
remember, my soul, to grow upon thy grave. Two
small black steeds are grazing on the meadow, soon they
will canter gaily home to the town - and slowly they will
go when drawing thy corpse.

Der Feuerreiter (The Fire-Rider)   Wolf
The Fire-Rider is abroad on his galloping horse. The
mill is in flame and destroyed. After that horror the
horseman is seen no more. But the miller sees in the
burned ruins a skeleton horseman who collapses into
ashes. May he rest in peace!

Der Gärtner (The gardener)   Wolf
Upon her steed, white as snow, a beautiful princess
comes riding along. Little rose-colored hood, let me
have one of your plumes! In exchange I give you a
beautiful flower - I shall give you a thousand flowers!"

Der Genesene an die Hoffnung (The convalescent to hope)
Wolf
The convalescent who, in despair, abandoned hope of re-
covery is hopeful once more.

Der Mond hat eine schwere Klag' erhoben (The moon complained) Wolf
The moon complained and accused you before the Lord;
she does not want to stand in Heaven, as you have
robbed her lustre. When she last counted the stars,
the two brightest were missing: your eyes, which are
blinding me.

Der Musikant (The musician) Wolf
I love to wander. I sing beautiful old songs, outside,
barefoot in the cold and never know where I will sleep
the night. Many beauties find me pleasing - but I am
such a poor vagabond. May God bless you with a husband who can offer house and home. If we two went together, I should never sing again.

Der Tambour (The drummer) Wolf
If my mother could hypnotize she'd be a canteen woman.
At night when no one is up but the guard, and all snor-
ing, I'll sit before my drum. My drum must be a bowl
with warm sauerkraut in it; my drum sticks will be
knife and fork, my saber a sausage and my shako a
stein full of burgundy wine. The moon shines in my
tent and I dream of my love; alas my game is ended by
the moonlight! If my mother could only hypnotize.

Die Bekehrte (The converted one) Wolf
Roaming through the woods at sunset, I spied Damon
blowing his silvery flute. He drew me close and kissed
me bold and sweet. Now he is gone, but his song haunts
me still.

Die ihr schwebet um diese Palmen (Ye that hover around
these palm trees) Wolf
Ye that hover around these palm trees, your vigil keep;
ye holy Angels, silence the breezes! My Babe is asleep.

Du denkst, mit einem Fädchen mich zu fangen (You think, to
catch me with a little thread) Wolf
Do you try to catch me with a little thread and to set my
heart aflame with a look? Don't trust me when you see
me laugh. I am in love, but not with you.

Elfenlied (Song of the Elf)   Wolf
The night-watchman shouted, "Eleven o'clock." A little
elf woke up. Drunk with sleep he thought someone was
calling him. He saw the glow-worms on the stone wall
and mistook them for lighted windows.
"I'll look in," he decided, "it must be a wedding there."
And he hit his head on the hard stone. Well, Elf, did
you have enough?

Er ist's (It is he)   Wolf
Spring flings her azure banner, and perfumes waft once
more their fragrant wings. Violets in the ground dream
of early waking. Spring is here at last! Spring is
come!

Führ' mich, Kind, nach Bethlehem! (Lead me, Child, to
Bethlehem!)   Wolf
Lead me, Child, to Bethlehem! Thee, my God, I long
to see. Come, sweet Saviour, lead Thy servant unto
Thee.

Fussreise (Wandering)   Wolf
With fresh-cut staff, I saunter forth at dawn o'er hill
and valley. Oh that my life might be full of effort un-
tiring as a perfect morning's wandering!

Gebet (Prayer)   Wolf
Lord, send me what Thou wouldst of joy or sorrow, I
am content that both should come from Thy hand.

Gesang Weyla's (Weyla's song)   Wolf
You are Orplid, beautiful isle, shining in the distance;
from your sunny beaches ascends the mist which wets
the cheeks of the Gods. The eternal waters, while ca-
ressing you, are regaining new youth! Before your divin-
ity kneel the kings who are your servants.

Gesegnet sei (Blessed be the Lord)   Wolf
Blessed be the Lord who created the world. He made
the ocean, He made the vessels which are gliding over
its surface. He made the Paradise and created beauty
and your sweet face.

Heimweh (Home-sickness)   Wolf
He, who has to leave his country, should take his beloved with him. The stars are shining - as they did when
I went to see my beloved. I listen to the nightingale's
song - the same song I heard around my beloved's home.

In the quietness of the morning I climb the highest mountain - to greet you, home!

Herr, was trägt der Boden hier (Lord, what does the soil bear?)   Wolf
"Lord, what does the soil bear which you water with your tears?" "Thorns which will be twined into wreaths for me and blossoms for garlands for you."

Ich hab in Penna einen Liebsten (I have a lover in Penna) Wolf
I have a lover in Penna, another one lives in Ancona and one resides in Casentino, the next lives with me in the same place, four I have in La Fratta and ten in Castiglione.

In dem Schatten meiner Locken (In the shadow of my tresses) Wolf
In the shadow of my tresses, fast asleep, my loved one lies. Shall I wake my love? Ah, no! With care I combed my curling tresses in the morning, but in vain is all my trouble, the wind soon entangled them! Tresses, blown by soft winds, have lulled my loved one to sleep. Shall I wake my love? Ah, no! He must tell me that his grief is past enduring, that my brown cheeks give and take life. "Vixen" he has called me - yet he falls asleep in my presence. Shall I wake him? No!

In der Frühe (At daybreak)   Wolf
No sleep has cooled my eyes! Through my window I see that day is dawning. My mind is distressed with anguish that I find neither peace nor rest, but only alarming dreams. Doubt thyself no longer, troubled spirit! Courage! From every steeple you hear the morningbells.

Klinge, klinge, mein Pandero (Sound merry, my lute)   Wolf
Sound merry, my lute; yet my heart is heavy. Would you know of my suffering, all your tones would mirror my grief. While I dance, I feel the pain in my heart and my song is full of anguish - my thoughts wander to another one.

Lebe wohl (Farewell)   Wolf
"Farewell!" You do not know what this sad word means; you said it calmly and with a light heart. Farewell! A thousand times have I spoken this word to myself - 'til it broke my heart!

Lieder Der Mignon (Songs of Mignon)   Wolf
1. Heiss mich nicht reden (Bid me not to speak)
   Bid me not to speak, bid me silence, for I might open
   myself to thee - only an oath is on my lips and God a-
   lone can unseal it.

2. Nur wer die Sehnsucht kennt (None but the lonely heart)
   None but the lonely heart can know my sadness, alone
   and parted far from joy and gladness.

3. So lasst mich scheinen (Think me the angel I soon shall
   be)
   Think me the angel I soon shall be; let this white robe
   enfold me still! I hasten from this earth to seek a
   dwelling dark and chill, then shall I cast my snowy garment away. Though I dwelt with careless mind, I felt
   my heart with sorrow wrung, from grieving make me ever young.

4. Kennst du das Land (Knowest thou the Land)
   Knowest thou the land where the citrons bloom? Where
   from azure skies the breezes gently blow. Dost thou
   know it well? Dost thou know the house and marble
   statues? Knowest thou the mount? There lies the way.
   O Father! let us go.

Mausfallen-Sprüchlein (Mousetrap verses)   Wolf
   The child walks around the trap, speaking; "Tiny guests,
   tiny house, dear Miss or Mister Mouse, do come over
   tonight, when the moon shines! Close the door carefully
   and watch your little tail! After dinner we will sing and
   dance! My old cat may join us, do you hear?"

Mein Liebster ist so klein (My lover is so small)   Wolf
   My lover is so small that, without bending, he sweeps
   the floor with locks atrailing. While walking through the
   garden he is frightened by snails, and flies, and bumble-
   bees. A plague on all things humming, whizzing and all
   who make one stoop so low for kissing.

Mir ward gesagt (I was told)   Wolf
   For what distant lands art thou starting, beloved? Fain
   would I know the hour of thy departure that my tears
   might speed thee on thy way. Ah, think of me, do not
   forget, my love.

Mühvoll komm' ich und beladen (Sad I come and heavy laden)
Wolf
   Sad I come and heavy laden. Lift me up, Thou Helper

Holy! See, I come in hot tears with humble gesture, all
dark from dust of earth. Thou canst make me like a
lamb, white as snow. Thou dost pardon the offense of
him who repentant holds fast to Thee. Lift then, Lord,
the load I bear! Let me imploringly kneel before Thee,
that I over Thy feet, incense and tears may pour, like
the woman whom Thou forgav'st so that her guilt like
smoke vanished! Thou who told the dying robber: "Thou
shalt this day be with me in Paradise!", lift me up,
Thou Helper Holy.

Nachtzauber (Miracle of the night)   Wolf
    Night's enchantment, brooks murmuring, still woodland
    lakes, nature's solitude. Visions of beautiful days to a
    heart wounded unto death by love. Oh, come once more
    into the silent trysting place!

Nimmersatte Liebe (Love never satisfied)   Wolf
    Love is like that. Its thirst cannot be quenched. It has
    strange moods. Tonight we kissed until our lips were
    bleeding, but we seemed never to have enough. Love is
    like that - even the wise King Solomon loved in this way.

Nun lass uns Frieden schliessen (Let us make peace)   Wolf
    Come, let us join our hearts in renewed love and under-
    standing. Too long we've striven in bitter feud. Princes
    and kings make peace; then, shall not those who love,
    yield to each other?

Nun wandre, Maria, nun wandre nur fort. (Now wander,
Mary)   Wolf
    Now wander, sweet Mary, nor fear. The cocks begin to
    crow and the city of Bethlehem is within sight.

O wär dein Haus (Oh, would thy house)   Wolf
    Oh, would thy house were made of glass, my love, so that
    I might gaze upon you with all my soul. My heart would
    send more glances to you than the drops of rain that fall.

Schlafendes Jesuskind (Christchild asleep)   Wolf
    Son of the Virgin, heavenly child, sleeping on the wood of
    sorrow that the master gave you as a pillow; if one could
    see all the visions behind that brow! Son of the Virgin,
    heavenly child.

Schweig einmal still (Keep silent)   Wolf
    Keep silent, unpleasant, noisy creature. Detestable is
    all your hideous singing. Should you go on till morning,
    you would sing no pleasant song. Silence, I say! I'd

rather hear a donkey's serenade.

Storchenbotschaft (Message from the storks) Wolf
The shepherd sleeps in his barn on the heath and would
not change his pallet for the king's bed. He does not
respond to any knock in the night. Only once, when two
storks - husband and wife - tapped at the shutters, he
opened his door and heard the happy news they brought
from the Rhineland about his sweetheart and her baby.

Über Nacht kommt still das Leid (At night grief comes quietly) Wolf
At night grief comes quietly; with tears and sorrow you
greet the morning. At night comes happiness which
makes the bad dreams disappear when the morning
comes. Joy and grief come at night; soon they leave
you, to tell the Lord how you coped with them.

Und willst du deinen Liebsten sterben sehen (If you desire
to see your dying lover) Wolf
If you desire to see your dying lover, then do not bind
your hair. From your shoulders let it fall about you,
resembling filaments of golden sunshine floating through
the air. Your hair is lovely - lovely are you!

Verborgenheit (Secrecy) Wolf
O World, do not tempt me again with the illusion of
love's joys. Let my heart, in lone seclusion, hoard its
rapture and its torment.

Verschwiegene Liebe (Secret love) Wolf
Tender thoughts of love float over mountains and valleys.
If only one maiden would know who thought of her - my
love is as silent and beautiful as the night.

Was soll der Zorn (Why this anger) Wolf
Why all this jealousy and hate, my dearest? I have done
nothing to deserve it! Ah! rather take a knife and
come to me and put it through my breast! But if not a
knife, then a sword - that my blood may spurt heavenward! And if not a sword, then take a dagger, that I
may wash my pain in all my blood!

Wenn du, mein Liebster (When you, my dear love) Wolf
My dear love, when you come up to heaven, I will bring
my heart in my hand to meet you and we will throw ourselves at the feet of the Lord, who will forge our two
loving hearts into one in Paradise.

Wir haben beide lange Zeit (We have been silent a long time)
Wolf
> We had been silent a long time - suddenly speech returned to us. Love's angels flew down and brought peace again after strife.

Zitronenfalter im April (Butterfly in April)   Wolf
> The cruel April sun has awakened me - the May butterfly - before my time; thus I must perish and May will never see me in my festive yellow robe.

Zur Ruh, zur Ruh! (To rest, to rest)   Wolf
> To rest, tired limbs; to rest, and to close the eyes! It is at night that light comes back to me. Oh, guide me securely, you inner powers, to the light of deepest night. Oh, to be away from earth's suffering and, through night and dream, to find mother's heart.

Zur Warnung (Warning)   Wolf
> It is early morning, the poet wakes up after a glad night with a bottomless thirst. He is in poetic mood and calls for his muse. She comes and shouts out a nonsensical song. The poet gets frightened and finds that only wine can help him in this situation, and in a hoarse voice sings, "Please, you tearful singers, do not call upon the gods when you have a hangover."

WOLFF
> Wolff was an Austrian pianist, accompanist and composer. His songs have a melodic attraction and are well suited for the voice.

Alle Dinge haben Sprache (All things have speech)   Wolff
> Since your coming, all things have found speech. The earth, the sea, the sun, the harvest fields are all reborn! Oh, I must kneel and kiss the earth, stretch my arms to the sun, and shout to the sea!

Du bist so jung (You are so young)   Wolff
> You are so young, so lovely - I am like stone - so cold - so old - so tired. You give me roses to make me happy. You are so still and alone - well, take me and my roses and do what you want!

Es werde Licht (Let there be light)   Wolff
> The voice of God sounded in the gloomy night, "Let there be Light," and behold there was light - the splendor of your eyes.

Knabe und Veilchen (The boy and the violet)   Wolff
O lovely violet, bloom a while longer and become even
more lovely. I'll pick you for my loved one, that should
make you happy. The violet answered, "When you smell
of my fragrance, you will love me."

Meine Lebenszeit verstreicht (My life is passing away)   Wolff
My time of life is quickly passing away; I have not long
to live. Beloved, before I depart, let your lips bestow
upon mine my last comfort.

Soll ich denn sterben?   (Must I die then?)   Wolff
Even though so young, must I die? If my father, my
mother and my sister knew, they would grieve themselves
to death. If my sweetheart knew, she would die with
me.

Stimme im Dunkeln (Voice in the dark)   Wolff
What is the sound in the dark? The wind?   My blood?
I think a heart is somewhere beating.

Index by Title

179

184

193

Index to Songs by Composers

203

208

215